Global Quality

Global Quality

The new management culture

John Macdonald and John Piggott

MERCURY

First published in 1990
by Mercury Books
Gold Arrow Publications Limited
862 Garratt Lane, London SW17 0NB

Reprinted 1992

Coventry University

Set in Palatino by Phoenix Photosetting, Chatham, Kent
Printed and bound in Great Britain by
Mackays of Chatham PLC, Chatham, Kent

British Library Cataloguing in Publication Data

Macdonald, John
    Global quality.
    1. Executive management
    I. Title   II. Piggott, John
    658.4

ISBN 1–85251–039–0

PO 1513.
412198

This book is dedicated to friends at the Golden Fleece in Shaw, Wiltshire. They provided the fuel to keep us on the road.

Authors' preface

This book is designed to help all those managers in business and the public sector who are interested in quality and the future success of their organisations. The book is about managing in a different way. It sets out to demonstrate the need to change the current management culture, discusses the principles of quality management and finally provides a guide to the successful implementation of a quality improvement process.

The book is written in the everyday language of management, for it is not intended to be an academic treatise or a textbook on statistical methodology. However, the contents are based on considerable research and the combined experience of the authors.

What about the authors, then? How do two people write a book? Our friendship and quest for knowledge began with sharing our separate experiences in implementing total quality management. We also shared a belief that no one quality guru was the fount of all wisdom. Our collaboration on the book is based on discussion, and indeed argument, about the structure and content of each chapter. This approach initiated more research and discussion, and when we had collectively found all the words John Macdonald sat down and put them in order. In the text, the word author in the singular refers to John Macdonald.

Our friendship and collaboration has survived this ordeal. We are now associated, with other colleagues, in consulting and in teaching the concepts we have developed. We still learn and argue, but happily somehow always reach decisions rather than compromises.

John Macdonald
John Piggott

Autumn 1989

Contents

Part One – The Need To Change

Part Two – The Principles of Quality Management

Part Three – The Actions

PART ONE

The Need To Change

*The competitive need for Total Quality
Management. The global market
challenge. How to recognise the need to
change in your company.*

1   The quality challenge

There can be few current business or industrial topics which warrant the word survival as the measure of their importance. But the need for quality management is so great that executives must see it in that light. Western managers can see the evidence all around them.

Little more than thirty years ago Japan's 5,000-year-old society produced goods which had an international reputation for shoddy mimicry. Japanese cars, radios and other household and industrial goods were modelled on American and European products, but the modelling was only superficial. Component failure was endemic.

Today things have changed. Goods from Japan (and from many other countries who have learnt the lesson) have a well-deserved reputation for delighting the customer with excellence. The workers who produce them are among the highest paid, and their managers the most efficient, in the world. Japanese factories employ the very latest technologies, often setting examples to the very nations which originated the ideas on which those technologies are based.

What made the difference in just thirty years? Quality – or, more specifically, elevating the management of quality to the highest priority. The Far East woke up to its industrial shortcomings and dedicated itself to the production of quality goods.

What gives quality such importance is simply this: make goods or provide services which consistently delight the customer and your reputation will soar. Make goods which fall below customer expectations and almost without exception your customers will flock elsewhere. Much of Western industry today has a management problem – it is not competing efficiently in world markets – and it needs *total quality management* if it is to survive. There must be a total commitment to quality at every level of industry, beginning with top management.

But let us go back to Japan. The changes in management style and strategy which made the Japanese quality revolution effective did not come easily or immediately. It was not until Japan's businessmen and educators had spent considerable time in the West, studying competing management philosophies, quality control, business practices and consumer needs, that the way forward became clear.

The Japanese observed that quality was important, particularly in the United States, but it was being achieved in a self-defeating manner. Instead of planning for total manufacturing efficiency, US industry was investing ever more heavily in sophisticated 'quality appraisal' control, concentrating its effort on finding the defective goods *after* they were manufactured. As money became tighter, the high cost of appraisal developed into the idea of 'optimum quality' – the best quality that could reasonably be achieved in given circumstances. The Japanese (guided by two American gurus, Deming and Juran) were quick to see the inevitable consequences.

The West continued with its conventional wisdom. Quality control has remained the province of production, which establishes acceptable levels of quality and then sets up elaborate and costly controls and test facilities to find all the bad items that have been purchased or produced. But most of this activity is akin to closing the stable door after the horse has bolted. If the quality process had started with the customer, marketing and design, the majority of the bad items would not have been produced in the first place. To the conventional view of quality a lavish dose of self-deception was added; slogans like 'Buy American' or 'British is Best' only disguised the fact that both nations urgently needed to improve the quality of their goods and services even to maintain their share of world markets, let alone increase it.

Consequently the Western share of world markets has steadily declined. There has been a widespread penetration of Western home markets in cars and electronic consumer goods. It is well advanced in machine tools, and is growing in the construction and service industries. Now it comes not only from Japan but from developing countries like Taiwan, Korea, Singapore, Indonesia and Brazil. And it does not rely on underhand financial measures or 'dumping', but on high and consistent quality. It is not wicked foreigners who are creating this crisis, but Western consumers who want these products because they do what they were designed to do – every time. Western industry is reduced to persuading governments to impose import restrictions and urging the competition not to satisfy demand but to voluntarily restrict its exports.

The challenge is clear for all to see – if they have eyes that see and ears that hear. The Japanese (according to Department of Trade and Industry statistics) now have more than a 50 per cent share of world trade in the following:

Shipbuilding	Magnetron tubes
Zips	Cameras
Colour cathode ray tubes	Plain paper copiers

Video cassette recorders

Ceramic packaging for integrated circuits

Micro direct current motors

64K RAM CMOS memories

Radio remote control services

Electronic music generators

Electronic wrist watches

Numerically-controlled machine centres

Hi-fi equipment

Compact laser disc players

Ceramic capacitors

Some resistors, coils

Switches and filters

Electronic typewriters

Electronic calculators

Robotics (in the widest sense)

Tape recorders

Micro-electronic ovens

Satellite ground stations

Facsimile telecopiers

Artificial leather

Motorcycles

Pianos

Magnetic tape

Liquid crystal displays

Many managers still find it difficult to believe that the main challenge to the West is really based on quality. Surely, they say, our management and workmanship cannot have declined to that extent. In one sense, that is true – it isn't so much that the quality of Western goods had deteriorated but that the competition has set new standards of quality. These new standards have changed the customer's perceptions and heightened his expectations. Western industry has actually continued to improve, but world competition has increased at a faster rate.

Western industry can be likened to a group of youngsters playing football among themselves. The game becomes an enjoyable exercise and they easily fall into the temptation to ignore the rules of the game. Offsides and penalties are overlooked for the sake of having a good time. After all, what do referees know? And in any case, rules only slow the game down.

But now the same group plays football against a side which is playing to the rules – exactly. Now every kick, every move is important and all of a sudden the original group realises what football is all about. To add to the shock, the spectator (consumer) likes the 'new' football played by the rules. The West's leading international competitors are playing commercial football by the rules. Rules which the West invented. Western industry (like the youngsters) can go on playing the quality game ignoring the rules. However, though they may find it enjoyable for a time, very soon no one else will play with them and there will be no spectators.

The enormous intensification of world competition during the last thirty years has added another dimension to the quality challenge.

Quality is now a global issue. As Dr Feigenbaum has noted, 'Quality operations in an increasing number of companies and governmental programs today are becoming international in their outlook and scope.' Dr Deming stresses that 'we are living in a new economic age.'

More and more companies are now organised internationally. Operational, marketing, product design and thus quality decisions are integrated internationally. Parts, materials and services are now routinely sourced worldwide. Inter-government negotiations are now increasingly concerned with product liability and quality. The philosophies, systems and techniques of quality management are becoming a 'lingua franca' of government and international trade.

Clearly, therefore, quality management is important and many companies in the West are taking quality very seriously. Nevertheless, many managers are not giving quality a sufficiently high priority. Why is this? These managers' view of quality is similar to many people's view of China: they know it's there, they know it's important, but they have never paid it a visit. It is 'out of sight, out of mind' and so never fully understood.

The 'China Syndrome' management begins to pay attention to quality when market share falls, customer complaints grow or the cost of after-sales service escalates. They send for the quality manager (after all it is his responsibility!) and instruct him to launch a quality improvement programme. Marketing assists by providing the most creative promotions and communications staff to enthuse all with the need for quality. Quality improves, the promotions manager wins an award and everybody relaxes.

With relaxation the management returns to its old ways, totally concerned with cost and schedules. Quality, once again out of mind, is no longer a priority. Standards drop and management laments that the modern worker is not what he was. But it is not the workers' fault: they can sense that management does not really care about quality, so why should they? But the problem is not just a lack of management commitment; you cannot become fully committed to something you do not wholly comprehend. The real issue is that executives do not understand quality and their role in its management.

So what is quality management? Dr Kaoru Ishikawa, a major contributor to the development of quality management in Japan, states that it is a revolutionary management philosophy characterised by the following strategic goals:

1　Seek quality before profits.

2   Develop employees' infinite potential through education, delegation and positive support.

3   Build long-term consumer orientation, both outside and inside the organisation.

4   Communicate throughout the organisation with facts and statistical data, and use measurement as motivation.

5   Develop a company-wide system focusing all employees on the quality-related implications of every decision and action at all stages of development of the product or service, from design to sales.

These goals may appear simple on the surface, but experience shows that each requires a major commitment to change from top to bottom of the organisation.

Quality management demands change, but it is not in itself a static philosophy. It has been and still is steadily evolving to meet new challenges. There is nothing new about the control of quality, but only relatively recently has it had to be managed. Figure 1 traces the evolution of quality management. In one sense the modern emphasis on every individual's contribution to quality is a return to the day of the individual craftsman. He exercised personal control over a large proportion of the finished product. It carried his stamp and reflected his pride. However, there is a major difference; today's worker enjoys only a limited control over the systems that produce the total product.

At the turn of the century the work of efficiency expert Frederick Taylor and others brought mass production and the breakdown of the work process into small components of the whole. The worker lost identity with the final product, so quality had to be managed. Inspection became a work process in its own right, and increasingly became a tool to hammer the workers. Taylor's ideas extended Adam Smith's concept of specialisation and division of labour past the point of diminishing returns.

In the 1930s the teachings of Walter Shewhart of the USA and Edward Pearson of Britain introduced the use of statistical control charts and industrial standardisation to manufacturing. The use of these control techniques was accelerated by the massive growth in manufacturing brought about by the Second World War.

Two famed practitioners of this period, Dr Deming and Dr Juran, found themselves little heeded in postwar America. However, they were welcomed in Japan and from 1950 onwards made a major contribution to the Japanese revolution and the modern era of continuously improving quality.

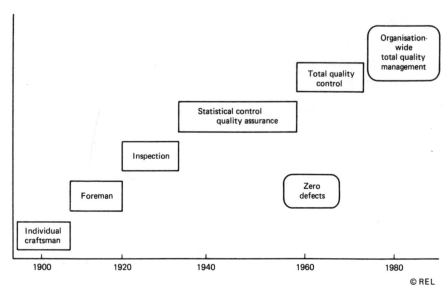

Figure 1 *The evolution of quality management.*

Until the 1960s the evolution of quality management was primarily concerned with manufacturing or operational processes. Armand V. Feigenbaum's book *Total Quality Control*, published in 1961, broadened the whole concept of quality management. Though his ideas do not go as far as Ishikawa's goals, he did influence the Japanese and quality professionals throughout the world. During the same period Jim Halpin's espousal of zero defects had only a limited impact, as it was misused by American management as a motivational tool to control the workforce. Philip Crosby's more general concepts, which include zero defects, began to have a powerful influence on both Western and Japanese management with the publication of his book *Quality is Free* in 1978.

For years the Japanese sat at the feet of Deming and Juran. Now they are sharing their experiences in published works and contributing new thoughts to the evolution of quality management. Notable among these writers are Dr Ishikawa, Professor Shigeru Mizuno and Genichi Taguchi.

In Figure 1 we looked broadly at the evolution of quality management concepts. The reader should not be misled by this diagram into believing that a substantial proportion of organisations automatically implemented these concepts within the time frames illustrated. Many companies are still back in the 1930s and the era of inspection. And even the

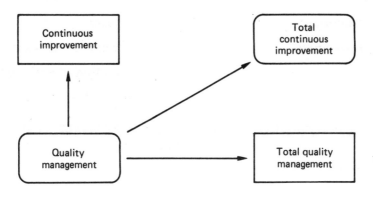

Figure 2 *A quantum leap forward.*

most advanced companies in the West are only now implementing these modern concepts into their non-operational areas.

Figure 2 represents the current mode of the majority of successful companies in America and Europe. They are working hard to eliminate defects in their production processes. The leaders among these organisations are striving in two directions. Operational management is concentrating on the reduction of variation and the continuous improvement of all the work processes. General management is involving the whole company in quality improvement. However, these efforts tend to concentrate on the elimination of defects. This is not to sneer at them, for they are indeed a major step forward. But if Western management is to achieve a sustained competitive advantage it needs a quantum leap forward.

The objective of Western management, for both operations and administration, is to move through total quality management (TQM) towards the goal of total continuous improvement (TCI) described in Figure 3. TQM can be seen as the process that is used to manage the change in environment that will ensure that the company reaches the goal of TCI. We need the TQM process to move organisations beyond the elimination of defects to the reduction of variation and to improvement and innovation.

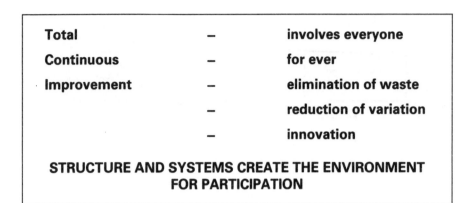

Figure 3   *The new objective – Total Continuous Improvement.*

This is a philosophy in which the instinct for improvement pervades the whole company – involving every employee. The Japanese have a word for this philosophy, *Kaizen*, which is most easily translated as continuous step by step improvement. This is what we mean by Total Continuous Improvement. This is the need; this is the quality challenge.

2 How far can the sun rise?

A lot of nonsense has been written about Japan. For twenty years correspondents have vied to find a single determinant in Japanese culture or business organisation to account for their success. The resulting misconceptions can prove a real impediment to the implementation of the best of Japanese ideas in Western business. In any case most of these ideas are Japanese applications of concepts that originated in the West.

An early facile misconception illustrates the point. For a long period Western management believed that the quality circle was the key to the quality revolution in Japan. They ignored the fact that quality circles were not widely used in Japanese industry for nearly two decades after it embarked on the journey to quality. Quality circles were established at work-group level to encourage volunteer workers to find ways to improve processes.

Quality circles initially appealed to the 'quick fix' mentality of Western management. They also supported the theory that bad quality was the fault of the workers and allowed management to delegate problem solving. The workers certainly knew the problems, but 80 per cent of them could only be addressed by management. Quality circles are a powerful tool if there is a receptive management. The environment, or management style, has to be changed before they can be effective. Their comparative failure in the West led to other explanations of Japanese success – and other misconceptions:

Japanese business is status free. This myth has appeared in a number of books and articles about the Japanese miracle and quality management. I sometimes think that the unstated desires of these writers cloud their vision or their judgement. The truth is that the Japanese are among the most status-conscious people in the world. There is a tightly ranked hierarchy in most Japanese organisations. Executive and management perks are the norm and are highly sought after in Japan. The Japanese may pay attention to communication in the workplace, but that is not the same thing.

All the Japanese companies are quality models. Whilst Japan has made astonishing progress in quality management, nobody is more concerned than the Japanese at the number of companies that are far behind the leaders. Their export industries are usually models, but others are as bad as Western companies. Mizuno has said that 'the tendency is to proclaim the successes whilst hiding the failures.' An interesting point arises from Professor Mizuno's examples of why some Japanese companies have more trouble than others. The reasons for failure are almost exactly the same as those in Western companies. Perhaps we are more alike than we realised. We will examine the issues of failure and success later. Social misconceptions about the reasons for the success of Japan abound in the West. A few are worth brief examination.

The Japanese worker is docile. There has been a period of relative calm in industrial relations. However, before believing that this is an integral part of Japanese culture those interested should read David Halberstam's account of the union battles of the fifties in Japan, in his magnificent book *The Reckoning*. There are signs that the rising aspirations of the people, unequal distribution of wealth, shifting demographics and land reform may herald a more difficult era in Japanese industrial relations.

The Japanese are workaholics. Certainly the Japanese employee works longer hours and takes shorter holidays than is common in the West, particularly in Europe. However, the current trend is towards greater leisure time and the five-day week is now an established fact. The younger generations are more avid consumers and are being influenced by Western thinking. The work ethic may become a decreasing advantage.

Lifetime employment brings lifetime loyalty to the company. This was never wholly true and in recent years mobility has increased, particularly among middle management. Lifetime employment never applied to the whole workforce. The cynical use of female labour disguised the real peaks and troughs in the business cycle. The headhunting profession is growing, and the proliferation of new businesses is eroding the lifetime concept in so far as it existed.

The removal of these commonly held misconceptions could help to reveal the differences that do exist between Japan and the other advanced industrial economies. Because Japan had a long history and a well-established culture before the quality revolution, consultants have argued that the concepts of quality management are culture-free. Whilst partially true, this view tends to oversimplify the problems of implementing many of the components of the quality improvement process. In the view of the authors, the structure and culture of Japanese business have made the application of these principles easier.

Peter Wicken, personnel director of Nissan Motor Manufacturing (UK), highlighted this issue in a book review in *Management Today*. He argues that Japanese companies are integrated and mutually supportive; that Japanese success lies in the synergy generated by a whole system and not in specific parts of that system. 'Western industrialists know the headings but rarely the detailed practice . . . just in time delivery of components can work in Japan because it is part of an integrated supplier-customer relationship where the supplier often has only the one customer, is wholly or partially owned and managed by senior executives of that customer and is located but a short distance from him. These conditions simply do not exist in Britain, where just in time can mean little more than transferring the inventory from the customer to the supplier's warehouse.'

Western management is compared unfavourably with its Japanese counterpart for its tendency to take the short-term rather than the long-term view. There is some truth in this assertion. But it is measurably easier to think long-term in a business climate where the synergy between big companies and the banking institutions is actively supported by the government. This is not the position in the West.

When all is said and done, none of these misconceptions or actual cultural differences should blind us to the fact that if the West is to remain competitive it must learn from the Japanese experience. That does not mean that we should wholly implement their approach without regard to our own environment. We should be distrustful of packaged solutions; our approach must be based on a full comprehension of the concepts of quality management and a clear assessment of our own needs. Above all we should remember two things: firstly, that most of the qualities we recognise in Japanese business are the direct result of corporate policies rather than the natural result of their culture. Secondly, that the Japanese originally learnt from the West and primarily from America.

The details of the techniques and systems associated with total quality management as practised in Japan are discussed elsewhere in this book. However, there are three key principles stemming from the Japanese experience that need special emphasis. These can be summarised as management action, *Kaizen* and education.

Management has the primary responsibility for quality. Common sense shows us that all work is a process, and statistical analysis indicates that over 80 per cent of defects in a process are due to common causes or the way the process is designed. Only management has the power, through control of resources, to change the system. People working in the process can usually solve the remaining 20 per cent of defects, which are special-cause problems. They can often *identify* the systemic problems, but are usually powerless to do anything about them without the support or help of management.

Management, therefore, cannot delegate the responsibility for quality. A moment's look at Ishikawa's goals (see Chapter 1), which lie at the root of total quality, underlines the role of management. They must set the policy and drive process improvement, and above all, their actions must support the integrity of the process of continuous improvement. This level of management commitment does not ignore the people, but rather the reverse. Japanese management talk of 'going to *gemba*', which roughly translates as 'the workplace'. This in practice is more than the 'walkabout management' now popular in some Western companies. It means going to the workplace and actively seeking co-operation and helping the workers to continuously improve. As Dr Deming says, 'The job of management is to help people do a better job.'

Kaizen has been mentioned before, but it involves such an important distinction between Japanese and Western approaches that it deserves special emphasis. The Japanese suggestion system or *teian*, actively involving the whole workforce, is a practical application of *Kaizen*, the process of continual improvement involving every employee. Workers participate in the suggestion system not only for the money awards that are standard in most Japanese systems, but for the satisfaction of using their minds and creativity every day to improve the place where they work and the goods and services they produce. This approach, first and foremost, builds the workers' morale and self-respect. It shows them that they are important members of the company, with ideas that matter. The company benefits from the workers' pride and high morale as well as from the aggregate financial benefits of the ideas they produce.

Teian has developed into a process quite distinct from the typical Western suggestion system. Rather than striving for a small number of 'stars' to come up with a few big ideas for saving the company a lot of money, the Japanese system encourages all employees to continually think of ideas, no matter how small, for improving any aspect of their jobs, not just cost.

A natural extension of *Kaizen* is the effort Japanese companies make to improve their employees through education and training. Peter M. Moir, in his book *Profit by Quality*, puts it this way: 'For Japanese employees, improving themselves is their most important job; process and product improvement will flow automatically from personal improvement. The idea of continued adult education for the employees would be received as anathema in the boardrooms of most, if not all, Western industrial companies, calling forth the most obvious objection,

"We couldn't afford it." Yet the fact remains that Japanese companies are not educating their employees out of any spirit of altruism, but for the hard business reasons that to do so reduces their development and manufacturing costs, increases their competitiveness, and increases their profit margins.' It also increases the general level of innovation, which is the cornerstone of their future success.

The Japanese employee spends, on average, 22 days of company time in education and training per year, and additionally spends an equal number of days of his own time training. The total of 44 days per year is several times higher than in even the best Western companies. It is time that Western management compared the cost of training with the cost of ignorance.

But let us return to the misconceptions. A major misjudgement about Japan is to believe that she is somehow immune to social and economic movements and pressures existing elsewhere in the world; that the inexorable rise in Japanese achievement has to continue *ad infinitum*.

The truth is that Japan is beset with problems at home and growing competition for world markets from her neighbours in the Pacific Basin. The danger is less that Japan will continue to dominate the world economy than that it will collapse domestically from the strains of over-rapid and unbalanced expansion. Japan survived these strains in the 1960s; it is not so clear that she will survive them as we approach the 21st Century.

The late eighties have seen a remarkable domestic boom in Japan. It has markedly increased the personal wealth of the one-third who own most of the nation's wealth, but at the expense of the two-thirds who produce most of the nation's output. A consumer boom thus based will put an intolerable strain on social and industrial relations. Consensus politics will end and confrontational politics will return. The impact this will have on participatory management and the integrated business structure can be envisaged. The 'them and us' syndrome, long thought to be a Western disease, could rear its head in Japan.

The competition will be waiting to take advantage. The rising sun may start to set again in the West.

3 Are the Yanks coming – or going home?

The Americans taught the Japanese how to put quality first, but paradoxically have suffered most from the change they spawned. American experts or prophets of total quality were spurned in their own country but welcomed with open arms in Japan.

The impact on the American economy has been swift and devastating. The table below, based on data from the US Commerce Department's Council on Competitiveness, highlights the nation's declining market share in products based on technology invented in the USA.

US-invented technology	1987 market size (millions $)	US share of domestic market (%)			
		1970	1975	1980	1987
Phonographs	630	90	40	30	1
Colour TVs	14,050	90	80	60	10
Audiotape recorders	500	40	10	10	0
Videotape recorders	2,895	10	10	1	1
Machine tool centres	485	99	97	79	35
Telephones	2,000	99	95	88	25
Semiconductors	19,100	89	71	65	64
Computers	53,500	NA	97	96	74

For the first time in US history, American children are unlikely to be able to live as well as their parents. The burden lies squarely on American industry; unless it improves quality and increases productivity the famed American standard of living will go into serious decline. It is being tenuously maintained by the massive trade and budget deficits, but you cannot go on mortgaging the future indefinitely. Indeed, the situation is in reality worse than that. The money being borrowed for consumption today will be unavailable tomorrow for investment in people and technology.

A noted American contributor to the debate on quality, Dr Jay W. Leek, said the following while discussing American quality in the *Best on Quality Year Book 1988*: 'We just didn't have any comparison with other countries as we do today. Now the average American is someone sitting in their home constructed of Chilean cypress and Japanese steel, sipping Brazilian coffee out of an English Spode cup, and nibbling Swiss cheese. He has probably just returned from seeing an Italian movie in his German car, powered by Arabian oil. He's sitting at a Scandinavian desk, writing a letter to his congressman on Irish linen stationery with a ball point pen made in Hong Kong, asking "What has happened to our balance of trade?"'

So how have American industry and business reacted to this shock to the system? Well, there is no shortage of expertise – the gurus have returned home and have become latter-day saints in their own country. Quality-management consultancy and education must be one of the fastest-growing business sectors in the United States. There certainly has been a change, but many American companies are finding it hard work adapting to the new emphasis.

The very best American companies – those which really understood that a deep cultural change in attitude and management style was required – have been successful. They are effectively competing on equal terms in world markets. They are world-class quality companies. They are proof that it would be unwise to write America off, and lament the decline and fall of another empire.

Hundreds of organisations in the USA are now implementing quality improvement in one form of another. These include service, manufacturing and public service organisations. Most are at the elimination-of-defect stage, however, and have not yet made a full commitment to continuous improvement as understood in Japan and the leading Western companies.

One interesting factor is the strong co-operation between companies engaged in the process of quality improvement. Often they are companies in direct competition; in other words there is recognition in the United States that quality is a global issue. Some of the most successful companies have established their own 'Quality Institutes' and are heavily involved in teaching the concepts of quality management to students from other companies. 3M have taken this further and act as consultants to other companies. Managers who have been particularly successful in implementing quality in their own operations are temporarily seconded to other firms to advise on the implementation of total quality management.

Personal observation suggests that there are aspects of American management culture which could hinder progress, in many companies, towards total continuous improvement. Their managers are superb firefighters and have a well-earned reputation for a 'get up and go', 'action this day' approach to business issues, but for all their easy first-name *bonhomie*, tend to manage by fear. (It is no accident that one of the American quality guru Deming's key fourteen points for management is 'drive out fear'.) Many rush to implement decisions or ideas without much prior thought in order to demonstrate to their bosses that they are dynamic and committed. This haste is not really their fault, as they are driven by short-term numerative objectives and an obsession with the numerate measurement of people.

The antithesis of this approach, empowerment of the people, is a new doctrine in American management circles which could prove equally dangerous. The problem is not so much in the concept itself as in its application by an ignorant management. Both approaches are based on a complete misunderstanding of the roles of workers and managers in the management of work processes. In both cases management are administering quick cures without any diagnosis of the apparent ills. Management needs to look at its current systems in the same way as a doctor looks at his patient.

These approaches will be examined in greater detail in Chapter 11. All of these tendencies mitigate against the careful planning and high level of employee participation demanded by total quality management. There is a real need for a change in management style.

Nevertheless, the United States is making great strides to regain its competitive edge. Europeans, for all their envy of America's role of Western leadership, may feel more comfortable following the emerging practice in the USA, rather than copying Japan.

Finally, we should remember that the Americans have been there before. Thomas Peters, in a foreword to James Harrington's book on the improvement process, observes that 'The Europeans were historically the craftspeople, from Holland to Germany. Among them, the British were the inventors, taking far more than their share of the scientific prizes. And the United States? We were the Japanese of a century ago: the copiers and perfectors of mass production.'

4 Old enemies or new friends?

In 1992 the nations of the European Community (EC) will have virtually completed their evolution into a United States of Europe. The removal of trade and customs barriers between these countries will create a single market of some 320 million people.

This market will help Europe to compete with the size of America and the Pacific Basin. But the EC nations have a two-thousand-year history of internecine strife for the domination of Europe. Will old enmities lead individual nations within the EC to expend their energies inwardly, rather than unite to exploit their common external opportunities? Will Germany, France, the United Kingdom or even Italy become dominant in the new market? Will there be a Japan of Europe using the single market as its base?

There are no easy answers. Certainly, there is a substantial divergence of views within Europe as to the degree of, and the pace of progress towards, unification. Equally, there is substantial co-operation between the individual countries on both political and economic fronts.

Many of the issues that currently divide Europe derive naturally from the history of the individual countries. West Germany's preoccupation with the EC's future relations with Eastern Europe and with the hope of recreating the Fatherland is an obvious example. Britain's fear of a Brussels Bureaucreacy slowing down her own dramatic social and economic revolution with a return to consensus politics is understandable. Because of her present opposition to the European Monetary System (EMS), with a common currency and a single European central bank, Britain may revert to her traditional divide-and-rule approach to the continental powers. As one might expect, France has her own attitude to the EC. In the time of General de Gaulle she vetoed the entry of Great Britain. The cynical British believe that France is using the EC as a great milch cow to mollify her farmers while she accomplishes her industrial revolution. The EC is governed by the Treaty of Rome so the Italians can feel proud, but they also feel a little left out as their giant neighbours to the north fight out the issues.

There are many other issues to be decided, but probably none that could reach the intensity of the 'divided we fall, united we stand' question 19th century America faced in forging her own United States. Most of the European divisions relate to the preservation and protection of national sovereignty. The author's viewpoint is that sovereignty is a little like virginity; once you have lost it you wonder what all the fuss was about!

Sovereignty, interestingly enough, leads us directly to quality. The whole subject is about delighting the customer. His perceptions when acting as a consumer do not recognise sovereignty, as Jay Leek's American example illustrated. Admonitions to 'buy British' play little part in most customers' buying decisions; they are interested in performance that will satisfy their needs as individuals rather than in the level of domestic content in the products they buy. It is not the wicked foreigner, but the wicked indigenous consumer, seeking good value without regard for the balance of trade, who is changing our perceptions.

So how is Europe reacting to the global competitive challenge of producing quality goods and services? There are differences in attitude and sense of urgency across Europe, but generally it is a positive story of co-operation and unity of purpose. Europe is actively learning from both Japan and the United States. As a result it is making its own contribution to the implementation of total quality management.

In recent years a number of surveys have been published on the issues of quality in Europe. Most notable among these are Mori's 1987 survey 'Captains of Industry', commissioned by Crosby Associates UK; the 1988 Confederation of British Industry (CBI) survey into 'Productivity in Britain', carried out by PA Management Consultants; and the 1989 European Logistics survey investigating company attitudes towards the importance of quality and service, produced by management consultants Knight Wendling. All these surveys indicate the growing awareness of quality as a management issue, the direction European companies are taking and the size of the task facing some nations.

The Mori poll demonstrates the tremendous surge of executive awareness of the priority that must be given to quality, if their companies are to survive in world markets. But the results are disappointing when it looks at the actions really being taken. It would appear that too many organisations are prepared to delegate the issue, or are seeking systems answers, rather than facing up to a real cultural change in the company. However, initial awareness is the first step towards recognition of the need and comprehension of the solution.

The intention of the Knight Wendling 'Logistics/Quality and Service' report was to explore the emerging changes in what European managing directors, chief executivies and general management focus on as the key to competitive edge in the 1990s. The companies surveyed operated across Europe in a wide variety of industrial and commercial market sectors, and included organisations such as Alfa Laval, Audi, Black and Decker, Boots the Chemists, British Aerospace, British Alcan, British Telecom, Carlsberg, Federal Express, IBM, National Magazine Company, Opel, Ohmeda, Rank Xerox, Reynolds Tobacco, Jacobs Suchard, Telenorma and Texas Instruments.

The report reveals a substantial change in the demands made on industry and commerce for improved quality and service. Its key findings are an interesting reflection of the changes in Europe:

- 93% of the European companies responding to the survey said that their customers were more exacting and demanding than ever before. The requirements for both quality and service had reached unprecedented levels, not just amongst consumers but within commerce generally.
- 94% are currently running quality improvement programmes in their company.
- 92% believed that quality problems occurred at all stages of the logistics process – not just during production.
- 73% of companies responding said that they had a formal procedure for measuring their customers' perceptions of the quality of their products and services.
- 89% of the companies involved compared themselves against the quality of services and products offered by their major competitors.
- 54% extended this comparison to see how they rated against companies operating in other industries.
- 63% had initiated customer awareness/care programmes within their company.
- 52% have recently changed and improved the management of customer service control in their business.
- 73% are putting greater emphasis on the task of controlling logistics within their company.
- 50% said they will rationalise the responsibility for company-wide quality improvement and the control of logistics into a single management responsibility.

The Knight Wendling survey reveals that there is a changing corporate view of quality. While the traditional response that quality meant 'conformance to customer requirements' was given by several customers, a more dynamic and forward-looking approach is evident in

European industry. Beyond the least rigorous definition of quality as 'meeting customer requirements', there was a progressive scale of company responses which included the following definitions:

- 'the positive characteristics which distinguish us positively from the others' (Jacobs Suchard)
- 'a never-ending improvement process of each individual throughout the organisation, from the top to the bottom' (Opel)
- 'the commitment of the total organisation to superior quality in product design, manufacture and service to achieve complete user satisfaction' (Black and Decker)

Virtually all the survey respondents had implemented one or more quality improvement programmes covering a wide range of functions within the company – product development, design, manufacture, sales, customer service, distribution and customer-care training.

The objectives of such programmes, however, varied in scope with the individual company's definition of quality. For example, those companies which defined quality as simply 'conformance to customer requirements' were likely to undertake quality improvement programmes to eliminate wastage and reduce production costs. Companies with a broader vision of the role of quality, however, had objectives like these:

- 'Make every employee a quality champion' (Black and Decker).
- 'Create a differential of excellence which sets the company apart' (Boots the Chemists).
- 'Instead of quality control or quality control parameters as a measure for quality, use the price you have to pay for not meeting the quality requirements' (Opel).

Between these responses there was a range of other objectives, which included:

- 'right first time, every time' achievement
- compliance with the highest level of market acceptance
- seeking a competitive edge through quality
- 'delighting the customer at all levels'

Finally, the research exposed several differences in attitude towards quality and service across the main markets surveyed, namely Benelux, West Germany and the United Kingdom. The most marked differences were these:

- While 100% of British respondents felt that there was a marked increase in demand for quality and service, only 88% of West German-based companies felt that this was the case.
- Nevertheless, 95% of companies based in West Germany have initiated quality improvement programmes, compared with 91% in Britain.
- Although the majority of companies in all the countries surveyed compared themselves with companies in the same industry, nearly two-thirds of German and Dutch respondents also compared themselves with leading companies in other industries; only one-third of UK companies did this.
- UK customers were perceived to be more influenced by price than other European customers – 82%, compared with 65% of German customers.
- UK customers were also perceived to be more concerned with quality – 82% of UK customers were seen as influenced by quality, compared with 65% of Dutch customers.
- Only 30% of Dutch companies planned to change the way they organise customer service activity, compared to 63% of the German and UK companies.
- All countries strongly denied that the majority of problems arose after the product had been manufactured, but there were diverging views on the point at which things started to go wrong:

	UK	Netherlands	Germany
Customer specification	14%	–	4%
Production design	8%	26%	46%
Pre-manufacture	22%	16%	4%
Manufacturing	30%	16%	24%
All stages	11%	32%	12%

In summary, the results point towards an encouraging growth, in Europe, of company-wide commitment to a quality improvement culture which is based on better communications both internally and with the customer to ensure that companies get it right, first time, every time.

The CBI survey puts Britain's productivity increase into perspective. British productivity is growing rapidly, but UK companies are not about to overtake their major competitors. This survey shows that if the rate of growth per person was maintained at its 1983–87 level, it would take Britain nearly ten years to catch up with France and West Germany, more than twenty years to overtake Japan, and the idea of catching up the United States could safely be forgotten.

There are some indications that this pessimistic report is not comparing apples with apples. These countries do not all establish productivity measures in the same way. For example, dispersed production in suppliers with a heavier labour content may not be included. Nevertheless, and perhaps more worrying to the British, several years of improving productivity and competitiveness have not got rid of the collective inferiority complex still affecting much of British industry. Less than one-fifth of the companies surveyed thought that they were world class. A few years ago, surveys such as this one would have been greeted with resignation. But Britain is improving her competitive position, and given the present mood in the country, this report may be taken as a spur to action rather than an excuse for giving up.

The report does indicate that the second stage of Britain's economic resurgence is going to be tougher than the first, and that was hard enough. Drastic and long-overdue changes have produced impressive gains in productivity and paved the way for seven successive years of continuous economic growth. The country is now taking the first steps towards catching up with its competitors. There is no case for complacency about its economic revival, no grounds for thinking that it can take a break. But it should be recognised that the best of Britain's improved industries are very good indeed. British Steel, for instance, is now the lowest-cost steel producer in the world, lower even than Taiwan, Japan or South Korea. It is also judged to produce the highest quality steel. A company which ten years ago was Europe's biggest ever loss-maker is now its most profitable steel company. All Britain needs is to continuously maintain the will to improve.

Britain has one major advantage that Japan can never equal – geography, the basis of its original success. Britain is twenty-one miles across the Channel from a market of 320 million people, and across the Atlantic ocean from a similar-sized market. Britain can return to her traditional trading success across the Channel and the Atlantic Ocean. She is closer to these two gigantic markets than Japan is. It is also worth noting that Britain has greater mineral resources of coal and oil than her Pacific competitor. She has a resource second to none in her people, too; citizens of the UK are powerful workers when they choose to be, or are allowed to be. Several well-documented cases exist of companies run by Japanese management with British workers that compete with the world's best. Once again the moral is clear: quality and productivity have to start with management.

Dick Wilson, author and expert on the Far East, found some encouraging answers for UK managers when he questioned Japanese managers working in Britain. These Japanese executives agree that the pervasive complacency of the past is disappearing from British industry: 'British industry has a rosy future, particularly since you have the flexibility of character and an international background,' says Wilson. He reports that a Honda executive went home questioning the belief that Japan had taken the lead in engineering. The executive told his compatriots that this belief might prove premature. He had discerned among the British a depth of understanding of technology and engineering which indicated a potential capacity to leap forward.

Professor Ryataro Komiya published a report in Tokyo entitled *Stagnation in West Germany and Advance in Britain*. He argued that German management was too secretive. In Britain he found the general level of management, technology, research and development and economic policy higher than in any other EEC country.

Ian Williams, business correspondent for the *Sunday Times*, reports Nissan as stating, 'Despite the rapid growth and new workforce, [our] new UK factory's quality is as good, if not better than anywhere else in the world, including Japan'. Williams says that 'the set-up there has encouraged Nissan's parent company to speed up development'.

Leading British industrial firms like ICI and BP clearly understand that total quality management is vital to their future success or even survival. The extent of this feeling is shown by the existence of bodies such as the British Quality Association, the Institute of Quality Assurance and the Department of Trade and Industry's National Quality Campaign. The latter now forms an integral part of the 'Managing into the 90s' campaign launched in 1989. The National Quality Campaign was lauched in 1983 with advertising telling the executive, 'Quality is too important to leave to your Quality Manager.' Part of the Campaign's objective has been to encourage companies to seek certification against the British Standards Institute's standard BS5750 on quality systems. The government and many major corporations demand that their suppliers have this certification. Now managers are finding that, although certification does enforce the use of quality systems and establishes some goals, it does not change the attitudes or style of managers and people. The growth of quality management consultancy in Britain since 1983 is indicative of market need. The high priority now being given to quality suggests that Britain does have an outside chance of becoming the Japan of Europe.

West Germany is in an interesting position in relation to 1992 and the growing quality initiative. Her reputation for quality worldwide has been close to that of Japan. The obvious similarity is that both nations met catastrophic defeat in World War II, along with the virtual destruction of their industries. They not only had to re-equip their manufacturing base, but needed to find new depths of discipline just to survive in the immediate postwar period. In retrospect, both factors were to their long-term advantage. They faced the new competitive challenges with up-to-date plant and had the discipline to change their traditional systems. However, there were essential differences. Germany was able to call upon a long tradition of superlative innovative engineering. The Japanese had to learn in an area in which they felt less secure.

Japan has gone on continuously learning and improving, to the extent that it has now become a natural habit – *Kaizen*. The authors' view is that West Germany has until very recently tended to rest on its laurels. Her quality is soundly based on good engineering design which relates to the manufacturing process. Advanced basic design could also guarantee long product life cycles. But we have a distinct impression that the Germans have become somewhat complacent. Rapidly-changing customer needs are now demanding a flexible approach. This in turn requires a flexible management and workforce. German innovation may surmount this obstacle, but if it does not, the country could be sitting on the edge of a precipice. In general it appears that the Germans rely heavily on inspection, which could cost them dearly in the years ahead. They should look very seriously at the destruction of their much vaunted lead in the camera market – now dominated by the Japanese.

Turning to the economic front, the verdict of the *Economist* of 12th November 1988 is interesting:

'West German business seems pretty smug about 1992. Many companies reckon they are so good at selling to foreigners that the creation of a single EEC-wide market will mainly mean scope to sell more. Yet West Germans have some reservations, for there are plenty of snags too. Mr Kohl's government came to power in 1982 calling for deregulation and the dropping of state subsidies. It has not done enough of either to ensure that all parts of the economy are sufficiently fit and flexible to compete in the new Europe. Among the likely losers in a larger market are the heavily protected transport sector and telecommunications.'

Another worry is that a lot of people in the EC would like to throw up new barriers to trade between single-market Europe and the rest of the world. West Germany, the world's biggest exporter, stands to lose most from tit-for-tat protectionism.

France has been quietly preparing for 1992, while managing a revolutionary transition from a predominantly agrarian economy to a modern technology-based industrial economy. Massive investment in her infrastructure and energy production are transforming France. The paradox of a government elected on a socialist ticket exercising Thatcherite policies is only part of the enigma. France is also investing in quality education and implementation. Companies such as Bull, Aerospatiale and Credit Lyonnaise are leaders in quality management on any measure. France is a major contender on the global stage of quality.

The north of Italy – the industrial base of the country – has also made dramatic strides in the competitiveness and style of her quality-based products. Italy probably lacks the overall financial and political solidity to become a major contender, but she will certainly become an influence in the new Europe.

This chapter has looked at the divergent views and practices within Europe on the issues surrounding quality management. But to emphasise that the positive movement towards unity is more important than the national differences, one important Europe-wide quality initiative must be mentioned.

In September 1988 the presidents of fourteen leading European industries established the European Foundation for Quality Management (EFQM). They expressed their wish to create conditions to enhance the position of European industry's products and services in the world

© 1988 European Foundation for Quality Management

Figure 4 *Quality management as seen by the European Foundation for Quality Management.*

market by strengthening the role of management in quality strategies. EFQM will develop specific awareness, management education and motivational activities in close co-operation with other European organisations, aimed at companies rooted in Western Europe that are in search of quality management. The Foundation's leaders express the multi-faceted character of EFQM's activities in a distinctive diagram (Figure 4).

In conclusion, the evidence is clear that Europe has embarked on the long road towards continuous quality improvement. However, as Dr Leek reminds us, 'We need to emphasise that Europe has and will probably always consist of widely diversified cultures, languages, national characteristics, political systems and national focuses.' That is the subject of the next chapter.

5 Vive la différence

We have seen that there are substantial differences between the national cultures of Japan and the United States and between those of the countries that make up the EC. These cultural differences go way beyond the obvious differences in language. Yet the majority of quality gurus or consultants would probably agree with Dr Armand V. Feigenbaum, who wrote, 'Implementing [quality control] principles doesn't depend on geography or national cultural differences. It depends instead upon a clear customer orientated quality management process that people understand, believe in and are part of.'

All are agreed that total quality management involves a cultural change in management style and in the attitudes of all employees. They also argue that the concept transcends national cultures. The authors accept the basis of this theory, but believe that it can oversimplify the practical application of quality management. Too many companies have been trapped by this theory, to the extent that they have ignored the fact that total quality management demands careful consideration of cultural issues. The consultants, also, are so convinced that quality is culture-free that they offer packaged educational services which disregard national or industrial cultures.

Quality problems are rarely industrially, technologically or financially based; they can usually be described as management, communication or people problems. However, all three of these areas are heavily influenced by national and, perhaps even more important, individual company culture. Even within one company, operating in one country, there can be substantial cultural differences between the various locations in which the company operates. These differences can arise from geography, function or the history of a particular location. Try communicating the need for quality improvement to a successful and growing high tech operation in, say, Reading in southern England, and then try the same thing in the same way at a basic engineering plant in Liverpool which has experienced heavy redundancies. The results will tend to differ! Yet many companies make just this mistake when launching a quality improvement process.

Too many firms confuse what they want to be with what they currently are. Executives may agree that they want a highly participative culture, involving everyone in the company. But if they are a heavily unionised company with a long history of 'them and us' thinking, they are facing a very difficult problem. Their awareness, communications and involvement programmes will have to be carefully planned and may take a long time. On the national level, deeply ingrained attitudes to change and differing educational standards are key factors in planning both education of employees and the implementation of the improvement process.

International corporations and consultants are particularly prone to ignoring culture differences. A common understanding will not be achieved if those communicating have totally different terms of reference. This problem is most noticeable in videos and other educational media. The most glaring examples are perpetrated when the developer of these media, wrapped in his own national myopia, simply does not recognise a cultural issue.

Sporting and ethnic analogies which assist the student in one country have exactly the opposite affect in another country. Humour is another tricky area; peoples around the world do not laugh at the same things. Some countries use understatement as a style, whilst for others hyperbole appears to be the norm. Material developed for international consumption requires more thought than mere translation.

Some consultants can also make the implementation of total quality management appear very easy indeed. The syllabus of one four-day course in England, for example, covered everything from understanding need to the complicated tools of Taguchi, and promised the student that at the completion of the course he would be equipped to implement TQM. A somewhat ambitious objective for any one course!

Without wishing to deter the eager executive, we believe he should be aware that changing management style or the attitudes of employees is not an easy or quick process. After all, it has taken a long while to create the existing organisational culture. A good guideline for measuring progress is the old medical dictum, 'If it's not hurting, it's probably not working.' Taking the medical analogy further, it's worth remembering that most cures are based on a full and careful diagnosis. In a similar manner, management should carefully assess, or diagnose, the symptoms in their own organisation before commencing the cure, and then carefully read the instructions before swallowing the packaged tablet.

The contrasting approaches taken by consultants in assisting organisations with quality improvement are in themselves a cultural issue for clients. Figure 5 illustrates the two most common approaches taken by consultants in the TQM market. Both approaches generally provide value for money, in the sense that things do improve, and the money saved from the solution of problems generally well exceeds the fees. However, these schemes do not always meet the original expectations and delight the customer.

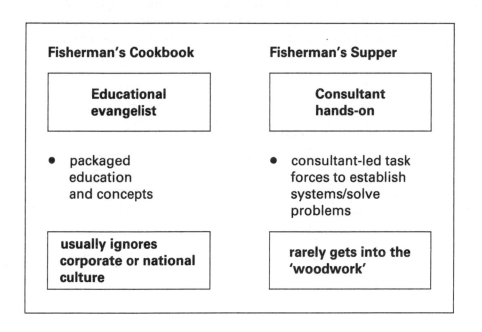

Figure 5   *Most common approaches to the total quality management market.*

The Fisherman's Cookbook approach, to the left of the diagram, relies on a packaged solution. The package is usually based on the works of one of the quality gurus. This approach does recognise that changing behaviour and attitudes requires education and a level of evangelistic conversion. But the approach is heavily reliant on standard videos and workbooks, and generally does not take sufficient account of the cultural differences we have discussed. There is also the risk that the client may receive insufficient 'hands-on' help in the initial stages of implementing the process.

The Fisherman's Supper approach, to the right, is more prosaic but does provide an immediate payback and a warm feeling. More often this approach is aimed at specific symptoms or problems rather than the whole style and attitude to managing quality. Its drawback is that it rarely allows the clients to take control of the process and make it his own. When the consultant departs there has been very little lasting cultural change; the process of continuous improvement has not 'got into the woodwork' of the organisation. This approach is more often provided by the generalist management consultants.

Figure 6 illustrates the authors' view of what assistance the client should expect from the consultant in implementing a continuous improvement process. In a sense it takes the best from both approaches in Figure 5, but it adds a synergy involving both the client and the consultant. This ensures that all education, systems development and communication takes full account of the cultural and organisational uniqueness of the client.

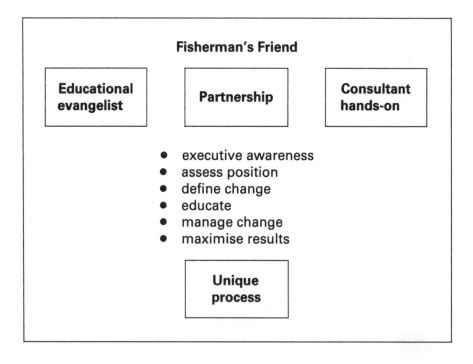

Figure 6   *What is needed in the total quality management market.*

The process starts with the education of the organisation's executives in the concepts of total quality management. Then the consultants work with the executives in a series of workshops to establish the principles and policies for quality that are best fitted to the company. During this period the company's position in relation to the six stages of quality improvement (see Figure 7) is assessed, the attitudes of employees are examined and a series of benchmarks or parameters for modelling the

The six stages of quality improvement

1. Assessment and awareness
Assessment of the company's need for quality improvement – of waste – of customer satisfaction – of employee attitudes – executive decision to change – communicating the need to change.

2. Organising for quality improvement
Establishing the quality management organisation – executive definition of objectives, policy, principles and values – establishment of the quality element of the business plan – establishing criteria and benchmarks to measure the process and resultant implementation.

3. Education
Educating and training all – providing competence in analysing work processes, measurement and process improvement. Focused on driving out fear, breaking down barriers and statistical thinking.

4. Establishing stable processes
Management-led analysis of key work processes – establishing customer, process and supplier requirements – establishing independent reviews for all products or services – implementing a company-wide improvement system – eliminating major problems.

5. Total involvement of all employees
Introduction of measurement by all work groups – establishing formal recognition – removing barriers to open communication – introduction of group-set goals in work groups.

6. Continuous improvement
Further analytical and statistical training of facilitators, managers and key employees – widespread use of statistical methodology – planned reduction of variation in all processes – introduction of other sophisticated tools – the whole organisation involved in *Kaizen* – continuous improvement of the process.

Figure 7 *The stages a company goes through on the road to continuous improvement.*

improvement process is established. The result is a company strategy and business plan to meet the chosen objectives.

Everyone in the company needs to be educated, according to either their role in the company or their role in implementing the process. Though the educational material will be generic to total quality management, the actual course material for both the instructor and the student will be developed to meet the special needs determined by the culture of the company, the nature of industry and the company's quality strategy.

The education and the strategy equip management to manage, maintain and steadily increase the effectiveness of the improvement process. The consultant helps by transferring his knowledge at each stage so that the process steadily becomes the company's own. The progress of change is continually monitored against the criteria established at the outset. The specific elements of this approach are developed in Part Three of this book.

This chapter was intended to warn the would-be student of total quality management about some of the initial pitfalls he might encounter. Those already involved in the process of continuous improvement may read this with a rueful smile. However, they will almost all tell the newcomer that careful assessment and planning are worth the effort. The road to quality improvement is a long one; it is not fully or clearly signposted and there are hazards on the route. Nevertheless, it is a rewarding and worthwhile journey. It can also be fun.

6 'You won't do it'

A Japanese executive told a British government-funded mission, studying quality in Japan, that he and his colleagues were prepared to share their secrets because ultimately they knew that the West wouldn't change. 'You won't do it,' he insisted.

This complacency could be Japan's Achilles heel. She has underestimated the determination of the West once before during this century. The West must accept the quality challenge and make history repeat itself.

The need to accept the challenge is clear. It is a matter of survival. The evidence is plain across the Western world. Ask the motorcycle manufacturers in Britain, the auto workers of Detroit and Birmingham, the television makers of most countries and the camera manufacturers of Germany. They were overwhelmed before the need was recognised. That's the negative side of the quality challenge.

There is a positive side. First, the West must fully understand the need and the nature of the changes she must make in the way her businesses are managed. All that is then required is to implement the process of change. A continuously improving West, dedicated to delighting its customers, will have a great competitive edge. The Western nations are still the most inventive and innovative on earth; allied to a Western version of total continuous improvement they will be unbeatable.

Total continuous improvement requires a cultural change. But what exactly is meant by cultural change? Dictionaries provide several definitions for the word culture, depending on the context in which it is used. The two somewhat similar definitions that apply in our context are:

- Culture is the *total* range of activities and ideas of a people.
- Culture is the total of the *inherited* ideas, beliefs, values and knowledge which constitute the *shared* bases of social action.

The second definition gives the clue as to why change is required. We have created a patina of inherited ideas and bad habits which obscure the obvious. Actually, most of the changes are commonsense. The first stage of the process is to dissolve the patina and look at our management principles and practices with a clear vision.

With clarity, we can see that our biggest problem is that we usually have several cultures within one organisation. Management and people, in Western companies, rarely *share the same values*, beliefs and knowledge. They do not have the same bases for action. The company is not working as a team towards the same objective. Figure 8 illustrates the needed cultural change. To engage in the total range of activities involved in the *Kaizen* culture, values and knowledge must be shared. The values are the operating principles of total quality management, and the most essential element of knowledge is a common language for communicating about quality issues.

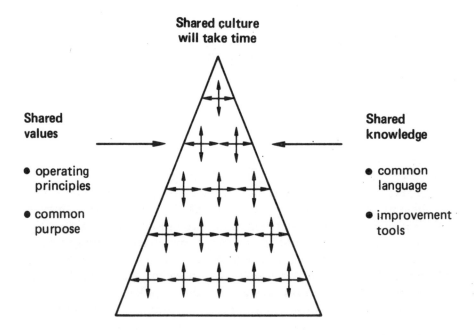

Figure 8 *Developing a shared culture for the management and employees of a company.*

Implementing cultural change is a process of education and coaching, as distinct from training. Everyone in the organisation must share in the education. However, they will also need skill training in the use of the tools of quality management. The specific skills will differ according to the roles people play in the organisation.

The educational process starts with the executives and senior management of the organisation. They must thoroughly understand the concepts of total quality management. Armed with this knowledge, they can develop the operating principles and values which will provide what Dr Deming calls 'a constancy of purpose'. All further education of middle management, supervisors and workers must include these same *organisation determined* principles and values. This requirement avoids the drawbacks of *packaged* quality-improvement education which may use similar but *foreign* (outside the organisation) principles.

The systemic and skill-training elements of total quality management are developed in detail in Part Three of this book. But before we decide to start this cultural change it will help if we fully recognise the need for change within our own organisation. We are more likely to achieve a constancy of purpose if we can fully understand and appreciate the need in our own backyard. That is the subject of the next few chapters.

7 It's them, not me!

At seminars, the authors have invited executives to rate separately the performance of business as a whole, and the performance of their own company, against a set of world-class quality parameters. Generally, eighty per cent of the executives rated their own company well above the national average. It is a natural tendency to see the faults in others before we recognise our own imperfections. However, until executives recognise the need for change in their own organisations they will not measure up to world-class competition. The future best-performing companies on the world stage are most likely to be found within the twenty per cent who are currently not satisfied with their quality performance. Striving to be best – that is what differentiates the world-class companies. They are not satisfied with the conventional approach to management. They recognise the need for objective assessment of their own performance.

The remaining chapters in Part One of this book are aimed at helping management teams recognise and understand the evidence from within their own companies that they need to change their management style. A recurring theme throughout the book is the central role of management in the pursuit of total quality. Unless management wholly accept that improvement is their responsibility, nothing will change. It is not a matter of motivating or cajolling workers to take quality seriously. Whatever their attitude, the workers are powerless to make any significant change without prior management action. Management itself has created this situation.

Management has spent most of this century taking power away from the workers. Mass production, and the concomitant complex organisation of work processes, has taken from the workers their influence on the product of their labour. Misuse of management power forced the workers to organise, through unions and trade associations, to defend their very existence on any reasonable level. Eventually, the pendulum swung to the extent that unions and management became locked in a stand-off, to the detriment of the customer. The business could no longer be managed. Companies turned inward; managing the organisation became more important than managing the business.

As the strife continued and organisations became more complex and cumbersome, the customer became more remote. The very reason for the existence of the business, the customer, was forgotten and in some companies he was perceived as an external hindrance to the smooth running of the organisation! However, the customer was not standing still during this period. His perceptions began to change. The customer began to organise through pressure groups and consumer associations.

This move was not exactly welcomed by the management of large organisations. Instead of viewing the consumer associations as a useful channel or sounding board to help them understand the changing needs of their customers, many companies saw these groups as an unwarranted interference in the flow of business. Now competition from those who did listen to customers, notably the Japanese, is at last forcing all companies to rediscover the purpose of business.

The introspective concentration on the needs of the organisation leads to many compromises in which quality, and therefore the customer, is the loser. Hierarchical management structures are reinforced by management-by-objectives and people-appraisal systems. Short-term financial objectives are driven down through the functional elements of the organisation. This encourages a fortress mentality in functional departments at every level. Each group, busy defending its own territory, is often oblivious to the needs of other departments in the chain which eventually leads to the customer.

A feeling that you are only as good as your last month's revenue or expenditure figures helps create an ambience of fear. It certainly concentrates the mind on individual departmental objectives, but at the expense of inter-departmental communication. Sales and production managers throughout the world recognise the power of the 28th of the month, which increases in intensity as each month passes. Every salesman knows that he can give concessions which will be supported by management on the 28th of December. Similarly, the production manager knows that quality is little hindrance to his shipping schedules at the end of the year.

The traditional claims that the garages of production and marketing directors were filled with product on the 1st of January is a joke, but nevertheless reflects an attitude. The vertical stress within the organisation is in direct opposition to the horizontal chain of work processes which create the final product. As Dr Deming continually reminds us, we must drive out fear and remove the barriers to communication. This subject will be more fully discussed in Chapter 11.

Fierce international competitive pressure has forced manufacturing companies to rediscover the customer and assess their ability to meet customer needs. The industry leaders are recognising the importance of quality. Management style and organisational structures are evolving to meet the new challenge. Few companies are yet near the TCI objective, but they are progressing. However, there are still thousands of companies in the manufacturing sector who have not yet got the message. And what about the service industries and the vast arena of the public sector?

In many Western countries service industries are the fastest-growing sector of the economy. Are they immune from the growing expectations of consumers? No, of course not, but the issues are not so clear. In financial services like banking and insurance, leisure industries such as travel and hotels, and to some extent retailing industries, the situation facing management is more confused than that for manufacturing industries. To begin with, the product is less tangible. Many services are produced and consumed at the same time. A motor car or a TV Set can be repaired or replaced if faults are found after it has been sold; customer esteem can then be recovered by continuing use of the product. What is the situation with the broker who fails to act in timely fashion to execute his client's order to buy or sell shares? How does the restaurant owner react to the customer who contracts salmonella poisoning, or the travel agent handle a disastrous holiday? At the extreme, to hammer home the point, what can the surgeon do when things go fatally wrong in the middle of a heart operation? 'After-sales service' simply doesn't apply; high compensation and a dissatisfied customer (or angry, grieving survivors!) is the inevitable result.

Traditionally, quality of product, or in their case prime service, has not been a major issue for the management of service companies. The evolution of quality management, discussed earlier, has not really applied to the service industries. This is understandable, because the operating process differs radically from that in manufacturing industry. There is no production line or process chain in the obvious sense; it is there, but the issue is clouded. The service (product) can be, and often is, uniquely provided by one invidual in the organisation. The traditional quality-inspection activities do not apply. Administrative support, such as invoicing, is similar in all industries, but we have seen that manufacturing industry with its quality bias rarely considered administrative functions as directly related to quality. Therefore, it is not surprising that service industries, being predominantly administrative, would not have taken quality so seriously.

Growing pressure from the customer and fierce competition are now forcing the quality issue to the attention of service companies. The need for some change is recognised by service management, but full comprehension of the nature of that change is still slow to emerge. Quality-of-service programmes tend to concentrate on the lower echelons of the organisation. They all too often suffer from the same drawbacks as the quality circle. In many cases they are little more than courtesy training – 'Be nice to the customer, we need him.' This is not to detract from courtesy, but it does not fundamentally change the organisation. Clearly, the differences in operation, history and attitude that set service companies apart from manufacturing industry create both obstacles and opportunities for the implementation of total quality management.

Professor John Oakland, at an international conference in 1988, highlighted three obstacles to the straightforward fulfilment of quality management principles in service industries. They can be summarised as follows:

1   The managements of service industries are, generally speaking, almost totally unfamiliar with the substance and business value of quality principles.
2   Investment in quality is viewed as an unnecessary expense rather than an investment with a payback. Quality programmes are seen as having a negative effect on productivity.
3   Customers are not genuinely listened to. Their complaints are often seen as an irritant rather than an opportunity.

These observations are undoubtedly accurate, though we would add that these same attitudes are not entirely absent in manufacturing industry. There is, however, a silver lining to these dark clouds. If the senior management of a service company can be convinced of the wrongness of the attitude that investment in quality is wasted money, then the first obstacle can become a positive advantage. Quality can be used as the strategic vehicle for change, for managers will not be inhibited by conventional wisdom on quality management, and there are no vested interests in inspection or quality departments.

The strategic issue is centred in Professor Oakland's third obstacle. The managers of service companies are divorced from their customers. This is not by design, but because of their low level of contact with customers. In most service companies the natural point of contact or 'interface' with the customer is at the lowest hierarchial level of the organisation. The senior management who define the strategy of the company have little natural interface with the majority of their customers. The following examples of the key interface with the customer in selected service industries will illustrate the point:

Banking	Bank cashier, electronic cashpoint or occasionally the bank manager
Restaurant	Waiter
Hotel	Receptionist/room service
Retail	Salesperson
Supermarket	Till operator
Railways	Ticket seller/ticket collector

The customers of these enterprises rarely meet the key decision makers. More important, the decision makers rarely meet the customers. This is the natural order of events. If management does not take specific action to communicate with these customer interfaces, it has no real contact with the changing views of customers. Generally the management of these service organisations communicate *to* rather than *with* people who function as customer interfaces. They attempt to motivate or even train these people at the lowest level to be nice to the customer, but they rarely ask them for their views of customer needs. The concepts of total quality management and total continuous improvement are heaven-sent instruments of strategic change for executives with vision in the service industry.

The public sector has a different set of problems in comprehending the need for quality. Public sector employees – civil servants – face problems in identifying the end 'customer' for their efforts. The absence of the profit motive, the lack of competition in the sense of an alternative supplier and the very nature of the product, which can be seen as a hindrance rather than a service, all add confusion to the common understanding of quality. Nevertheless, the sheer size of the public sector in advanced countries demands attention to these issues. For example, the National Health Service in Britain is the largest employer in Europe, with the sole exception of the Red Army.

In the broadest sense, the customer of the civil service is the general public, who as taxpayers pay the salaries and are the recipients of the service – or constraint. In a practical situation, the civil servant may well see his current political master, in other words the secretary of state or minister, as his customer. In the long run the political master is answerable to the general public, so the public-sector organisation can ethically accept that it serves that customer by serving the minister.

That this is a genuine concern for many civil servants is exemplified by recent prosecutions of public service employees in the UK over the release of information to the public that the government considered secret or confidential. The defence has been based on the 'greater good' concept, or the degree to which the public has a right to know. Freedom of information acts in the USA have highlighted this issue and perhaps point to the real customer.

Despite these fundamental differences between the public sector and industry or commerce, the deeper issues of management behaviour and attitudes of people are the same. Departmental fortresses and barriers to communication operate in a similar manner. The concept of the internal customer-supplier relationship applies to both public and private sector organisations. Government and civil service management are alive to these issues. It is perhaps a pity to observe that in the UK the drive to apply commercial disciplines to the public service has concentrated on the false gods of management-by-objectives and appraisal systems.

Most of the issues we have discussed in this chapter relate to the attitudes of management and workers to the customer. Underlying these issues are the attitudes of management and workers to each other – a matter of comprehension and communication. The following chapters are intended to increase understanding of all these issues as they apply within the individual organisation. To help management look inwards with some objectivity, the first step is to look outwards to the customers and their changing perceptions.

8 Who sold you that, then?

The real judgement as to the quality of a company's products or services is made by the customers. They decide whether or not the product meets their needs. Quality is not determined by the quality manager, the designer or the marketing department. Quality starts with delighting the customer. Recognition of the need to improve must begin with the company's perception of the customer and knowledge of the customer's perception of the company.

Many companies adopt and display facile slogans such as 'The customer comes first.' Very few have profound knowledge of what that statement really means. The authors' realisation of the importance of knowing the customer began with a simple exercise within a company embarking on a quality improvement process. To introduce the concept of the internal customer, managers were asked to conduct an experiment within their departments. Each manager led his group to select one of the department's internal customers. The group then attempted to define this customer's requirements. Then the manager, armed with a neatly typed list, visited the customer to discuss and agree the requirements. This exercise provided a major shock to the system. Up and down the company, managers found that their carefully prepared lists did *not* match the customer's requirements.

The point of the experiment was that each of the groups was enthusiastically putting the customer first. They wanted to please them and were happily determining their requirements. But they were wrong, and they did not find this out until they asked the customer. The external customers of the company are in exactly the same situation. Unfortunately there is rarely the opportunity to get it right next time – the customer simply did not buy and has now gone elsewhere. A world-class quality company really knows its customers and can use that knowledge to anticipate customer requirements. It never just assumes what the customer wants.

The business reader can carry out a simple test to determine to what degree the customer ethos permeates his own company. You are almost certainly the customer of the computer or Management information systems (MIS) department. Does their output satisfy your requirements? Have you ever received a computer-prepared management report with masses of data that has no applicability to your management needs? Have you had a meaningful discussion with the computer department to agree your requirements? If the answer to these questions is no, yes, no, then pause for a moment before blaming the MIS department. Their output may be symptomatic of other attitudes in the organisation. Many managers in large organisations consider that the only thing worse than attending management meetings is not being invited. In a similar vein, they also feel threatened if they are excluded from information which in reality they do not need. Quality, or meeting requirements, is often based on attitude; the primary attitude we need is to be customer oriented.

Customer perception has been helpfully summed up in the dictum, 'All customers want' – whether they are dealing with a bank, an insurance company, a retail store, a car dealer, or any other business – 'is what they have been promised.' Though this may not be quite enough to achieve a sustained competitive advantage, it is a useful starting point in examining relations with customers. All sorts of promises are made to the customer when the company is persuading him to purchase. The promises are often contradicted by the waivers contained in the small print after the sale. Promises are made in advertising copy, brochures, technical leaflets, packaging and in salesmen's statements. A senior executive in a service company picked up one of his own company's brochures and saw the statement, 'We practise what we preach.' He commented, 'I sure as hell hope that we do not preach what we practise.' Any organisation attempting to assess its customers' perceptions should objectively examine every promise it has made or implied through its customer interfaces. It should ask itself and give an honest answer – do we keep our promises in all respects?

Some industries seem to specialise in 'extras' – additional small items which the customer considers an essential accessary to the basic product. The quality of the prime product may meet all the customer's expectations. However, if on purchase the buyer is faced with unexpected charges for these extras or for a special service agreement, he will feel that the supplier has not kept the implied promise. The customer has a similar reaction to late delivery or incorrect invoicing.

The author has been a disappointed customer on nearly every occasion that he has purchased furniture or kitchen appliances. A relatively minor but decisive irritant when purchasing electrical goods is the failure of the manufacturer to include a plug so that the appliance can be immediately used, or even tested in the shop. Most retailers stock plugs and will supply them at extra cost, but will usually flatly refuse to fit the plug. The appliance will not work without a plug. The manufacturer's excuse is that he does not know the kind of power socket in the customer's home. There really can be no excuse for this hassle to the customer now that the vast majority of homes and appliances in the UK require a standard 13 amp three-pin plug. The customer who has a different system knows that he has that problem and will not be annoyed to receive a fitted 13 amp plug. The majority of customers would be delighted with a fitted plug. In most cases a basically good product has been 'spoiled for a happorth of tar'.

Manufacturers seem surprised that customers get so annoyed over little things. They are concentrating their attention and resources on the *significant few* defects to the extent that they tend to ignore the *insignificant many*. Yet customers are funny about these. They often face a delayed shock when making major purchases such as a car. They are so excited and delighted by the new buy that they are not looking for the little things. Then a small fitting falls off, one of the doors does not fit exactly, a small light on the dashboard goes, the central locking system omits a door. Now the customer, who was boasting to friends about the new car only weeks ago, is castigating the car manufacturer as hopeless. This is how the term 'Friday cars' entered our vocabulary. The major problem can be fixed and may soon be forgotten, but the many minor inconveniences are rarely fixed and remain as a constant reminder that the product does not meet expectations, and that therefore the manufacturer is not a quality company.

Western manufacturers were lulled into a false sense of security because for many years the customer's perception was that this was just the way things were and that you have to grin and bear it. But the customer's perception of quality has changed dramatically over the last decade. People have been shown another way, and they like what they see. The problem facing Western industry is not the wicked Japanese manufacturer, but rather the wicked customer who has been educated to expect products that work right first time and every time and do exactly what they are claimed to do.

Consumers are increasingly more sophisticated and demanding. The revolution of rising expectations is accelerating faster than the undoubted improvement in product and service quality. Consumers are more sophisticated in that they are more conscious of the total lifetime cost or real value of their purchases. They are more likely to consider product life and the cost of maintenance and after-sales service. Their expectations go beyond the specific product or service they buy. They now measure a company by the accuracy of the invoice, by the clarity of user instructions, by the accuracy and level of information on the packaging and by a host of other interfaces additional to the product. They are also increasingly aware of hidden benefits or defects surrounding the product. Environmental or health issues – once almost totally ignored, probably through ignorance – are now at the forefront of buying decisions.

Customers are also more demanding in the sense that they are much more likely to complain and insist on attention. The compliant, voiceless customer is a dying breed. In the past the small customer felt defenceless against the giant corporation and the big company took advantage of that situation. That era ended with the publication of Ralph Nader's book *Unsafe at any Speed*. Now the consumer is organised. He subscribes to consumer associations who represent, advise and educate him. News travels fast, but unfortunately for errant companies, bad news travels faster than good news. It can take a long while to win back a once dissatisfied customer.

The growing strength of consumerism is reflected in the attitudes of governments and the changes in product and service liability legislation. The common law legal dictum of *caveat emptor*, 'let the buyer beware', is almost a dead issue; it is now 'let the seller beware'. Though not new, the legal obligation of producers and marketers to compensate for injury or social loss caused by defective products has been strengthened and extended. The level of damages faced by manufacturers has escalated at an incredible rate, particularly in the United States. Society now takes a much broader and more onerous view of the manufacturer's responsibility for mishaps and tragedies resulting from the use of their products. Union Carbide may still refer to the Indian disaster as 'the incident at Bhopal', but society at large would use stronger words. Such incidents can bankrupt companies and sometimes damage whole industries, as the 1989 salmonella-in-eggs issue in the UK demonstrated.

These new consumer and social attitudes have landed the food processing industry on the horns of a dilemma. Negative reaction to the additives used for 'marketing' purposes, for example artificial colourants added to meat, has hardened to a call for the complete ban of *any* additives. However, many of the additives were developed by chemists in the food processing industry to protect the customer and prolong the life of food. This whole area has now become a tricky minefield.

In Europe the EC Commission has issued directives on product liability law which greatly strengthen the position of the consumer. EC members are now bringing their domestic law into line with these directives. The issue of product liability now extends far beyond the manufacturing process to cover the total operations of the company. Total quality management should now be viewed as essential for the survival of the company, let alone its future growth.

Many manufacturing and service companies measure the effectiveness of their quality performance by the level and type of customer complaints. Certainly customer complaints must be listened to and analysed, and they must lead to corrective action. However, complaints are a poor measure of product performance, and a low rate of complaints is not proof that customer expectations are being met. Earlier it was seen that the customer or the consumer association is now more likely to complain than in the past. However, many people still feel that it is not worth the trouble – the hassle associated with getting a meaningful response is a major deterrent. These customers complain with their cash by changing their supplier when their level of tolerance is exceeded, so only the most serious defects are actually brought to the attention of the manufacturer. The minor defects are rarely highlighted in a customer complaints report, so these reports give management an incomplete picture. By its very nature, measuring quality by customer complaints is a reactive process – a little like driving by looking through the rear-view mirror. It ignores the fact that in the fast-moving marketplace the customer's expectations are never static; they are constantly changing.

Customer complaints are, however, a valuable form of feedback and interface with the customer if properly handled. The response to the customer is in itself a quality issue. It can either enhance the complainer's view of the company or strongly confirm his suspicions. The very fact that he has taken the time and money to write or telephone may indicate a lingering desire to give the company another chance and continue trading. If he is then bounced from one telephone extension to another, or receives a standard reply some weeks later, it is often the last straw. Our objective should be to talk to customers to obtain the data needed for planning to meet their needs; make it easy for them to communicate with the company. Make it easy for them to be a customer. Senior executives should look carefully at how the company responds to the customer, and ensure that the organisation's systems and controls are designed to help the customer rather than satisfy the organisation.

The quality-conscious company will take a pro-active, rather than re-active, stance towards the marketplace. It will take positive steps to know its customers or consumer groups. It is amazing how few companies really identify their customers and attempt to establish their existing and future needs. Perceptions are a complex factor in the buying decision. Consider the speed at which products move from a never-before-seen innovation to a basic necessity of life, or business. The customer's perception or attitude to performance changes dramatically as the generic product moves through the cycle. Consider how the customer's perceptions and expectations have changed in just a few years regarding the following products or services, some of which did not even exist a few years ago:

Television sets	Microwave ovens
Facsimile machines	Personal computers
Video recorders	Cameras
Car telephones	Music centres
Air travel	Fast food takeaways
Retail shopping	Food safety

In some cases external social issues and behaviour trends will influence customer perception and attitudes towards a product. The successful company will always be looking ahead, anticipating these changing needs and perceptions. For many of the above products the original innovators are no longer the principal suppliers, and in the service area the dominant companies of just ten years ago no longer lead the pack.

The senior management of a company considering the need to change its quality culture must make an objective assessment of its position in relation to the issues discussed in this chapter. The data needed for answering the questions below may not exist within the company, so outside help in the form of research and surveys may be required. However, these questions cannot be left unanswered; the future lies in comprehension of the present.

Ten questions on sensitivity to customer needs

1   Does all the copy in our advertisements, brochures, technical briefs and packaging accurately and truthfully represent the service we aim to offer our customers?

2   Do our contracts, delivery notes or service agreements contain waivers or let-out clauses negating the implied or explicit promises we made before purchase?

3   What percentage of our field service or after-sales service manpower is spent on unplanned service or maintenance?

4   What percentage of our overall revenue is dependent on our after-sales service?

5   What standards have we established in the organisation for dealing with customers' telephone or written queries?

6   To what degree has our market share changed over the last three years?

7   How do we compare with our principal competitors (both at home and abroad) in terms of market share, growth, quality of product and quality of overall services surrounding the product?

8   Who in the organisation has the specific responsibility for defining who our customers are and communicating their present and future needs to management?

9   What is the level of our overdue receivables? (Propably 90 per cent of overdue receivables are a company's own fault through faulty communication with its customers.)

10 How many of the organisation's customers have you personally talked to over the last month?

9   Never mind the quality – ship it!

The competitive pressures for quality from outside the company are relatively clear. The competing pressures from within the organisation that militate against quality are not so apparent. These self-inflicted pressures are often so strong that it would be accurate to say that the company is actually organised to ensure that quality is *not* achieved.

Company management is typically measured against revenue, cost and deadlines. Quality is rarely used as a measure of senior management's performance. Within this environment quality is sure to play second fiddle. Quality is generally seen as a technical subject outside the realms of business decision-making. But quality is far too important to be left to the quality manager. It should be a principal concern of the whole management team. As Philip Crosby has said, quality must become first among equals with revenue, cost and schedule. It is the job of senior management to get all of these competing pressures in balance.

Most managers are totally unaware that their decisions and actions are actually causing non-quality to happen throughout the organisation. They would be horrified if such a suggestion were made to them and would cite many actions that they had initiated in support of quality – things like the new poster campaign and the recent leading article in the company newsletter. It would not occur to them that quality only appeared on the operating committee's agenda when there had been a serious problem involving a major customer or the level of customer complaints had jumped. These managers are not venal – putting quality first is just not part of the company's culture.

One of the authors was just such a manager. He held a variety of marketing posts, including Director of Strategic and Product Marketing in a major corporation, but to the best of his memory cannot recall quality being on the agenda of any general-management meeting. Quality was obviously discussed from time to time, but was never the driving force in running the business. He well remembers the shock when a wiser managing director asked him to fill the new post of Director of Quality

Management. His immediate though unspoken reaction was, 'What have I done wrong?' But the company was about to take quality seriously.

All companies should reflect on how seriously they take quality. This applies even to companies that have launched major quality improvement drives. Has quality become part of the everyday management culture of the company – is quality 'in the woodwork'? Some organisations have spent vast sums of money educating and training all their management and their people. An improvement-process organisation has been established. There is a company quality policy displayed throughout the organisation, and management is forever talking about the never-ending commitment to quality. The cost of quality has been reduced and there has clearly been an improvement in product and service quality. And yet deep down the culture has not really changed. What has gone wrong? In reality management has never wholly understood what commitment to achieving quality through people really means. The company will get the things that it rewards. The management and people are still tasked, measured and rewarded on the basis of revenue, cost and schedule. Quality has a high profile and it is a matter of concern and people are recognised for their contribution to quality. However, when the chips are down in the key areas, quality will be compromised.

What are the recognisable symptoms of a company driven wholly by revenue, cost and schedule? Where does the company compromise with quality? The symptoms are many and varied and they can be found at all levels and in all functions of the company.

Consider the launch of a new product. The scenario is not unusual. A major area of the company's product offering is close to the end of the product life cycle. All manner of 'mid-life kickers' have been employed to extend the sales life of the product. Special discounts are in force and new capabilities that strain the basic technology have been added. Sales volume is falling, profit margins are down and the costs to the field service operation are escalating. At this moment research and development announce that they are close to a technological breakthrough which could provide a replacement product with a vastly improved performance at a lower cost. A word of warning – the new concept has not yet been fully tested. Resource is required for design and engineering to produce a prototype to fully test the new approach.

Marketing receives this announcement as manna from heaven. It perceives a whole new niche in the marketplace which could radically alter the competitive position of the company. However, there is only a small window of opportunity. The new product must be launched within eighteen months. Despite the protests of design and engineering, marketing persuades the management team to schedule the launch date for June of next year. 'We must think positive and have faith,' declares the marketing director: the first and most costly compromise with quality. The tone has now been set and the culture established.

At the first design review before production is authorised (there was no time for a concept design review) a series of risks are highlighted, ranging from unacceptable through high to low. Engineering protest that they have not been able to test a fully viable prototype because of the continual design changes. Design counter that they were given insufficient time and resources to complete the design – 'You kept yelling for the drawings before they were finished.' Manufacturing are now realising with shock that the design changes will require a massive re-jigging and new machine tools. These are not in the budget. This interests finance, who order manufacturing to reduce the shop costs: 'See that purchasing get their act together – order in large quantities now before the projected price rises; find some new suppliers who really want our business.' Marketing are only slightly perturbed: 'If only the technical people would stop their wrangling and get on with the job.' Marketing are now very busy designing brochures and product briefs and discussing the advertising campaign with the agency. Time is now running short and the launch schedule is threatened. General management authorises full production. The compromises with quality are multiplying.

At the final product review before the official launch it is clear that everyone has been working very hard and a lot of time has been caught up. There are a few problems with the product, but they are not insurmountable – or so it appears. The product is a new computer system. At this stage it cannot handle quite as many terminals as originally specified, and response time is a little degraded. The original claims are now encapsulated in the brochures and product briefs, but marketing can warn the sales force, adding that 'in any case that will not really matter, as the customers are unlikley to fully load the system.' There are some bugs in the operating system, but software design know about them and will be providing fixes not long after the first installations. Systems test mention that they are meeting some reliability problems with the new cheaper chips that purchasing were able to get from a new supplier.

The field service representative is beginning to look rather worried. He was not able to attend the previous meetings because the engineers were busy firefighting with the old product. Finally, field sales found out that the technical installation and maintenance manuals are not complete and no engineering familiarisation courses have been organised. The field service rep tentatively suggests that the launch and first delivery dates should be delayed until all these *little* quality problems are ironed out. A hush comes over the meeting.

The marketing director is the first to break the pregnant pause and he explodes: 'We have booked a stand at the Birmingham National Exhibition Centre and the Duke of Edinburgh is coming in by helicopter . . . there can be no question of delaying the launch.' Both the managing director and the finance director look alarmed; they are both depending on the new product to lift the second half-year revenues. The company cannot afford to delay the new product. Launch and delivery dates are confirmed. The objectives of revenue, cost and schedule appear to have won again. Quality was not the first priority, and once again has been compromised. However, in reality – as time will show – so have all the other objectives.

The launch is a great success and the first systems are delivered on time to enthusiastic customers. A warm glow suffuses the company; IBM will now have to look to their laurels. The first draught of cold air comes from the field service operation and the next from the sales account managers. All the equipment has been delivered on time, but the final commissioning of the new systems has been continually delayed. The installation engineers are meeting new problems with the advanced technology. Incomplete training and manuals mean that much of their work is being completed by trial and error. The customers have started to re-examine the warranty clauses in the contract.

Excited by the specification of the new equipment, some of the customers have used the opportunity to redesign and expand their business systems. Now all the minor deficiencies from the original specification begin to take their toll. The sales order processing system of a mail order company is not able to utilise as many terminals as intended, and in any case the response times are slower than promised. Murphy's Law decrees that this is the largest and most prestigious customer. Senior management are involved and a more powerful processor and faster discs are installed at no extra charge. When another company attempts to use all the clever facilities in the new operating system it overloads the allocated space. The account manager provides more memory at no additional cost. Then accounts receivable bills the client for the additional equipment. Their invoicing systems naturally depend on the installation lists completed by field service. The account manager has forgotten to issue a credit note, or perhaps he was too frightened to get management approval for upgrading the equipment to viability. In any case the customer has not yet paid the original invoice because of the commissioning delays and his warranty claim.

Overdue receivables are leaping up, and at that moment the Chancellor increases interest rates. Now it's all the fault of the government. These problems will continue for a long time until the product 'beds down' and it is time for a new product launch. Next time, of course, things will be better! But in the meantime, what happened to those all-important objectives for revenue, cost and schedule when quality was compromised? All these communication issues and problems of divided objectives are illustrated in Figure 9.

Management by objectives (MBO) can be a very dangerous weapon in the armoury of modern management. Generally management use MBO to shoot themselves in the foot. At business school it all appears so logical and organised: people need to be set clear objectives, and they should not object to being measured against them. It is so logical that few question the initial premise. What kind of objectives? Well, obviously, the general objectives of the business, carefully broken down to apply to each function and level within the organisation. And what is the ultimate objective of the business? Any fool knows the answer to that question – profit, which comes from the careful management of the competing objectives of revenue, cost and schedule.

Progressive business schools or courses also teach us that the greatest resource of the company is people (the most expensive resource, hence a key factor in the cost objective) so we must nurture and educate them. We must avoid confusion and clarify the objectives for them, and for this activity we have designed a very special system called 'staff appraisal'. This system will be based on the same divisive objectives, but that is another story.

The terminology of large companies is very interesting in the context of quality. At the 'sharp end' of the company you are 'only as good as last month's figures'. We will discuss some of the attitudes this culture engenders amongst employees in Chapter 11, but first consider how this compromises quality. Reflect on how onerous the policies and procedures of the company become on the 28th of the month. On the 28th of December every salesman worth his salt at the 'sharp end' can invent his own disclaimers, discounts and special conditions. Particularly if his manager is below his revenue target.

This is not to say that business objectives are not important. Profit, revenue, cost and schedule are not only important, they are in fact part of the quality objective. The new reality is that management must perceive quality as the *prime* objective. If quality becomes the driving force, the other objectives will follow. The recipient of our product or service is the customer, and he has a choice. The lesson of the consumer revolution is that he is increasingly prone to choose quality. Meet the customer's objectives and the company will meet its objectives. This used to be called a fair deal.

From this discussion it can be seen that the implementation of a total quality management philosophy will require more than a quality policy, education and systems. From the outset the company must involve itself

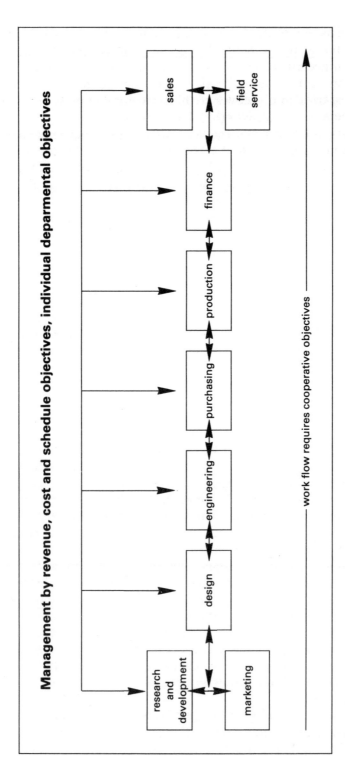

Figure 9 *Competitive pressures inside the organisation.*

in a careful assessment of how it sets objectives and communicates them to departments and individuals. The assessment should include the following questions:

1 Are departmental objectives short term, wholly numerative and divisive?
2 Do individual objectives create anxiety and fear or mutual trust within the organisation?
3 Do the objectives, policies and procedures of the company create barriers to communication between the departments or levels of the organisation?
4 Could any of the objectives, policies and procedures of the company be amended to engender communication and co-operation between all sections of the organisation?
5 Has the company ever compromised on quality because of the objectives, policies and procedures determined by management?

10 I know quality when I see it

The first time the author heard Philip Crosby make a speech, it was to an after-dinner audience of approximately one thousand people, primarily service engineers. He opened with the question, 'Is anyone here against quality?' He paused, but there was not a peep from the audience. He continued, 'I have asked that question a thousand times and nobody has ever answered me. Now here is a subject – quality – which everyone knows is important, everyone is for, nobody is against.' He paused again and then asked, 'If this is the situation the puzzlement is, why don't we *get* more of it?' This was a sobering point (it had been a good, convivial dinner) and was the real start of the author's conversion.

The point that Crosby was making was that eveyone knows what quality is, or certainly feels secure with his own view of quality. Unfortunately, these views differ and are usually subjective. Quality means goodness, or excellence, or 'I know quality when I see it.' These are not hard management facts such as revenue or cost. It is difficult to communicate through subjective opinion, and if the definition of quality is subjective it is impossible to manage. This is the major reason why quality is not a principal objective of management.

In many organisations the quality manager is not much help. He communicates quality through complicated indices of performance and customer satisfaction. This just adds to the confusion. Misconceptions about quality abound throughout the organisation. What is really needed is a definition for quality that can be used as a common form of communication throughout the organisation.

Most of the gurus and organisations or associations dedicated to quality have their own definition. The problem with these is not so much that one is right and another wrong, but just that they are different – rather like national cultures. The important issue is that the individual organisation should select or design its own definition so that it can form part of a common language of quality. The definition should be clear and leave no doubt in the mind of the users as to whether quality does or does not exist in any transaction.

Some of the more widely used definitions of quality are noted below:

Conformance to requirements	Philip Crosby
Fitness for use	Joseph Juran
The totality of features and characteristics of a product or service that bear on its ability to satisfy stated or implied needs.	BS 4778
The total composite product and service characteristics of marketing, engineering, manufacture and maintenance through which the product and service in use will meet the expectations of the customer.	Armand Feigenbaum
The degree of conformance of all the relevant features and characteristics of the product to all of the aspects of a customer's need, limited by the price and delivery he or she will accept.	John Groocock

The more long-winded definitions may well be accurate and extremely logical, omitting nothing from the equation. However, they are difficult to use as clear messages for communication to everyone in the organisation. The authors happily used Philip Crosby's definition for many years. It is clear and easily used to communicate quality to the whole organisation. It also has the massive advantage of being *binary*. In other words, the output from a work process either meets the requirements or it does not meet the requirements. Quality has been achieved or it has not. No doubt, no fudging. However, quality has moved beyond the elimination of defects – we are competing today in markets where improvement must be continuous and constantly adding more to delight the customer. The authors' own definition for quality is *delighting the customer by continuously meeting and improving upon agreed requirements*.

This is probably no better than any other definition, but it represents our current view. That is that quality relates to continuous improvement and that the people working in processes are party to an agreement to meet requirements. It also emphasises the customer. The requirements for quality in a product or service must reflect what will delight the customer, not what the organisation feels it is capable of producing.

Deming adherents strongly emphasise the limitations implied in the word *requirements*. Generally they believe that the use of this word leads a company to settle for simply meeting the specification. We have some sympathy for this view, but are strongly influenced by the imperative to translate customer needs into company action. For each internal supplier to meet an internal customer's requirement is a methodology for establishing the first link in Deming's chain reaction. The emphasis on continuous improvement of these requirements prevents the wrong attitude. No doubt this definition can also be continuously improved! Figure 10 illustrates the objective.

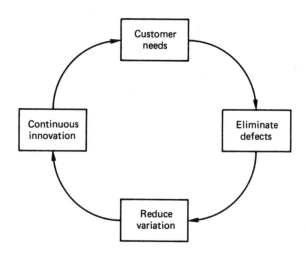

Figure 10   *The real quality circle – a customer-driven company.*

A major misconception about quality is that it is confined to the product, and therefore to the manufacturing process. Nothing could be further from the truth. We have already seen that the customer's perception of quality includes more than the satisfaction obtained from the primary product or service. Their view of the company that provides the basic need will include how their original inquiry was handled on the telephone, the method and timing of delivery, the clarity and helpfulness of the operating instructions and the timeliness and accuracy of the invoice. Clearly, if we are to delight the customer, quality management must be extended to the administrative areas.

Quite apart from these considerations, the actual manufacturing process does not stand alone. The evolution of quality management demonstrated how at first the measurement of inspection of quality was confined to the final product. Later the concept of the *process chain* was married to the concept of managing quality into the product during its manufacture (quality assurance) and led to the consideration of quality in the obvious earlier links of the chain, such as design and engineering. However, product quality depends on much more.

An example from the computer industry illustrates the point. At a certain factory some 44 per cent of the sales orders received were proved to be wrong in substantial elements. Not forecasts from marketing (the bugbear of every production manager) but the actual orders from customers. This led to incorrect ordering of components, wrong assembly of system facilities, subsequent rework, late delivery and customer anger. The issue was highlighted by the decision of the factory management to establish a duplicate sales order processing operation to check the orders received from sales order processing. Investigation into cause showed that sales order processing was making errors and that the salesman was incorrectly completing the original customer order, but neither situation was the root cause of the problem. Marketing had not properly maintained and communicated sales order option amendments and numbers to either the sales force or sales order processing. The salesman, sales order processing, marketing and the factory were all using different databases. The company had concentrated on quality at the factory, but it had never occurred to them to look at quality in the marketing, sales or finance departments. Yet the customer's dissatisfaction with the product stemmed from those areas.

Every company has non-manufacturing departments which are typically considered to be totally separate from the production line that is actually turning out the product. In manufacturing companies a substantial number of the employees are involved in administrative procedures. The whole manufacturing process depends on these 'non-productive' white-collar workers. Quality applies as much to their work processes as to the production line. Indeed, it could be argued that the imperative in these areas is even greater, if only because quality has to date been totally ignored in the administrative functions.

We have already seen how this blind spot in management thinking has pervaded the retail and service industries, where nearly 100 per cent of the employees can be classified as administrative. Interestingly, the word 'quality' is used to advertise the wares of service companies as much as, if not more than, the products of manufacturing companies. Yet the application of quality management to service companies is in its infancy as compared with the industrial sector. Quality is more generally seen as the smile on the face of the receptionist rather than the conforming processes which support the front office.

Similar thinking lies behind the misconception that quality is the responsibility of the quality manager and the quality manager's department. Quality is the responsibility of everyone in the organisation. It is more directly the responsibility of general management, because only they command the resources and the power to create the environment and provide the education and tools that everyone requires. The quality department manages some of the skills, systems, tools and techniques that can help the organisation. Measurement, testing, process inspection and establishing standards do not create quality, however. They are techniques for providing data to enable others to so manage the process that it produces conforming output.

Despite the evolution of quality management techniques there is one misconception about quality that still dominates management thinking, particularly in the administrative areas. Quality is innately perceived as separating the good from the bad. Quality is almost automatically associated with checking, verification, reconciliation, inspection and rejection. The whole objective is to prevent the mistakes or bad work reaching the customer. Total rejection of the bad is very expensive, so there is a concentration on fixing or reworking the defective goods or services. 'We can paint it on the lorry' is the attitude of far too many managers. These same managers would see themselves as having a high regard for quality and a customer orientation. After all, their activities are in the customer's interest. They are so busy checking and ticking boxes that they never pause to consider how an error happened in the first place. Ways to avoid the costs of this attitude will be examined in the next chapter. The real objective of quality management is to prevent the mistakes or bad product ever being made.

Management has a tendency to believe that increased productivity, efficiency or quality (and all three are closely associated) will be achieved mainly through investment in technology. Most certainly, investment is required in better machine tools, computers, automation, robotics and a host of other business equipment. However, all this investment will not necessarily achieve quality. In the days of the seller's market, computer companies waxed rich on the cry that computers improved efficiency. Computers have allowed companies to envisage and carry out tasks that were previously beyond them. However, there is little evidence that electronic data processing has inherently improved the quality of output from work processes. In many organisations they have added a further complexity in the inter-relationship of individual processes within the overall work flow. Indeed, a substantial number of the non-conformances in several processes can be attributed to the knock-on effect of errors originating in computer operations. Computers sometimes just distribute *problems* faster and more widely.

The reality is quite simple. Quality is achieved through people. People manage processes and people work in processes. People control machine tools, people programme robots, people put data into computers, people purchase materials and people manage people who manage processes. To effectively manage quality, the organisation has to work through the chain of people who work on and in processes. 'People', therefore, is not just a polite new term for the workers. 'People' start with the chief executive.

The people chain, and therefore quality, both starts and finishes with the chief executive. He determines the direction and the personality of the company. What the managing director believes is important to the business will influence his direct reports in establishing their priorities, and so on down the chain. This can be both a strength and a weakness in establishing a quality culture in a company. Such a culture cannot be achieved without the commitment of the chief executive. However, if he does not ensure that the conceptual reasons for his commitment are shared with the whole company, the quality culture will not permeate the woodwork. In that case quality can be likened to a hard gloss coat of paint without an undercoat or preparation. The cracks will multiply the moment the CEO puts down the brush – either diverted by another priority or leaving to join another organisation.

Sir John Egan, formerly of Jaguar, is a good example of top management's role in creating a quality culture. The quality of Jaguar cars improved rapidly because Sir John took quality seriously. Everyone in the organisation knew that his first question would be about some aspect of quality, so *everyone* took quality seriously. Only time will tell the extent to which the quality ethos has entered the fabric of the company.

The following questions will help you determine how far it has permeated your own company:

Questions on company understanding of quality

1 What is the company's definition of quality?
2 What is the company's quality policy?
3 Who is responsible for quality in your operation?
4 Are quality measurements used in the administrative operations?
5 How much time did you spend on preventing errors last week?
6 How much time did you spend on firefighting, rescheduling or chasing up orders or information last week?
7 What is the system for corrective action in your company?

11 Why doesn't he say what he means?

There are two key factors in most organisations which contribute to confusion, frustration and an awful waste of resources. Ultimately, they are the factors which result in non-performing products and services being delivered to customers. The first factor is the failure of managers to explain clearly and precisely what they expect from colleagues or subordinates. The second factor is the use of management systems which force distinct functional areas or departments to operate as islands unto themselves.

Both these factors are behavioural and stem from industrial history. They are born of early industrial theory and have been perpetuated by business schools and management consultants. Since the early days of the industrial revolution and the advent of mass production, management theory has tended towards the technical or organisationally systemic solution to industrial problems. It is not so much that the behaviour of people has been ignored, but that the natural first reaction of management has been to manipulate or 'motivate' the behaviour of workers to fit the current organisational system. When the system fails, the reaction of management has been to blame the people for being obdurate or not being as motivated as in earlier generations. Typical statements of the thwarted manipulative manager are easy to recognise:

'The workers are just bloody-minded.'

'People have lost the work ethic.'

'Workers just do not understand when they are well off.'

'Workers are no longer interested in quality.'

It would never occur to the managers who make such statements that even if they are true, the responsibility for such attitudes lies with them. Chapter 7 touched on the steady erosion of the individual worker's power to influence events in the workplace. This is a direct result of the organisational approach to management. It is a natural human behavioural pattern to react against or resist such a situation. Other pressures, such as survival, may lead the reaction to be relatively passive or, *in extremis*, lead to industrial anarchy. To be fair, not all managers share these attitudes and there is growing evidence of a change in management behaviour.

Companies are beginning to act as if they realise that people are their greatest resource. They are making that or similar statements in company publications. But it takes time to really change behaviour; old habits die hard. Tom Peters dramatically illustrated this dichotomy between what management say and what they actually do. In a televised video he produced a company annual report which extolled the importance of the employees' contribution to the company's success. Peters said that the *real* management attitude was to be found by noting which of the company's contributing people had names. The company report was lavishly decorated with photographs. Every photograph which included senior management mentioned their names in the caption. Other people featured were merely described as an engineer, a surveyor or a production worker. In other words, these lesser beings did not have names. That is the real message being given to the employees. In reality this is unthinking behaviour rather than culpable behaviour that is exhibited by all involved in producing and authorising the brochure. But the real point is that management behaviour does have to change and be seen to change. They do have to start thinking and acting in a different way.

Total continuous improvement will not be achieved until there is a change in management behaviour which will result in a change in the attitude of all employees. The first step in behavioural change is the establishment of a set of principles on which the change can be based. As the change is directly related to people, the principles must be supported by values which can be shared by management and workers.

World-class companies now take this issue very seriously. Companies such as IBM and General Motors give substantial emphasis in their management education to principles and values they want to see encouraged in their organisations. Perhaps the major lesson to be learned from the principles adopted by leading companies is that they have been individually developed to meet the prevailing cultures in those companies. Packaged principles selected from other companies or management gurus will have only limited effect. Everybody must be able to identify with the ideas being communicated, so they must be expressed in terms that relate to the culture in which the people have been reared. There is a very thin line between accepting that change is afoot and judging that this is just another motivational exercise.

The authors have developed a sample set of principles and values.

They are proferred with the admonition that each company should develop its own principles. The following statements, which relate to both management and people, may serve as useful models:

We recognise that our mission can only be achieved through people, therefore:

- We will treat each other with dignity and respect.
- We will communicate with each other in an open and frank manner.
- We recognise that all our people want to do a good job.
- We recognise that individuals want to know exactly what is expected of them.
- Individuals will be recognised for their contribution.

Our management are committed to continuous improvement, and they will lead by:

- Maintaining the constant purpose of the organisation and the improvement principles and values.
- Ensuring that there is a continuous programme of education and self-improvement for everyone in the company.
- Removing all the barriers that prevent improvement and open communication being achieved.
- Ensuring that all their actions demonstrate the integrity of the principles and values.

The company mission, the quality policy and the principles and values (of which the above form a part) should be regularly communicated to employees and displayed in all company locations, but establishment of principles is only the first step. All employees have to make them a living part of their daily behaviour. In every organisation the change takes time.

The present behaviour of people in a particular company and the culture of the company usually have been established over a number of years. It is worth noting that the resulting culture is rarely based on a defined set of shared principles, but it should also be said that it did not just happen by accident. The behavioural patterns of both management and workers were gradually evolved through the working relationships determined by the systems dictated by management for organising work. If management had wholly understood the systems they employed, the problem of the industrial divide – 'them and us' – would never have arisen. The way forward must begin with comprehension of these systems.

Shewhart and the industrial statisticians of the thirties preached the concept of variation in all things. A simplistic way of summing up these theories is to say, 'You cannot step into the same river twice.' The original river has flowed by and you are now stepping into a different set of conditions; different temperature, different speed of flow; different admixtures in the water. All has varied since you last stepped in the river. In developing statistical methods to measure variation so that it could be controlled and reduced, they demonstrated a number of simple truths about the manufacturing process. These truths were so simple that management ignored them. They were blinded by the complexity, in their view, of the mathematics involved. Some wrestled with the mathematics; most ignored both the mathematics and the simple truths. The statisticians bewailed the state of management training and declared that managers should be taught to be numerate. There is some truth in this viewpoint, but the statisticians must also learn to express the simple truths simply. The growing influence of Drs Deming and Juran on management thinking has occurred because they are expressing truths about management systems in a relatively simple way.

There is now no excuse for either management or statisticians. Calculators and computers can take care of the mathematics. Management can concentrate on understanding the simple concepts. Comprehension in this area will lead them to realise that the techniques they currently use for managing their businesses are actually diametrically opposed to the real dynamics of business operations. Businesses have more often succeeded despite, rather than because of, the way they are managed. Until the quality revolution there was safety in numbers. When *every* business was managed the wrong way, no one was found out. New competition has found the right way and soon there will be nowhere to hide; bad management will be found out in business failure.

An uncomprehending management has created confusion, frustration and awful waste of resources in an organisation. So what are these simple truths that they must learn? The implications for management of the truth that there is variation in all things will be examined later in the book. This chapter will concentrate on the following organisational truths which can unlock the present impasse:

1 All work is a process.
2 All work processes are interdependent and form part of a process flow.
3 All processes and all individuals are in a customer–supplier relationship.
4 People work *in* processes and management work *on* processes.

There is nothing complicated in any of these assertions; indeed they are commonsense. The changes in management behaviour that they demand are also only commonsense.

All Work is a Process

Work is simply an action or a series of actions that converts material or data into different material or data – a process which receives an input and produces an output. Two simple examples illustrate a work process:

Inputs	Work process	Outputs
Empty bottles	Filling shampoo bottles	Bottles of shampoo
Drums of shampoo		Empty drums
Survey report	Agreeing a	Agreed loan
Status report	mortgage loan	dossier
Client details		
Mortgage application		

Each process adds cost and should yield added value to the customer. These are simple examples of a process in action. A moment's thought will show that the first process will also require some machinery and a definition of exactly how much shampoo is needed in each bottle. The second process will require a calculator and a definition of standard terms for providing loans.

All Processes Form Part of a Process Flow

Usually the product or service purchased by the final customer is the result of hundreds or even thousands of individual interacting work processes, the outputs of one process becoming the inputs of the next process. Sometimes multiple outputs are necessary to form the next input. Similarly, one output may serve as an input to many individual processes (see Figure 11).

In real life the flow pattern is usually more complex (but not more complicated), with many activities going on in parallel and linking into a primary flow at different stages. For example, the final or external customers receive sales brochures from one flow line, place their orders in another flow line, receive product from a third line and their invoices from a fourth. The organisation of a business is a network of highly interdependent work processes (see Figure 12).

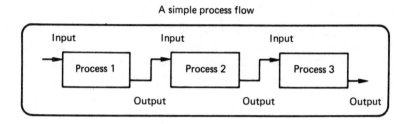

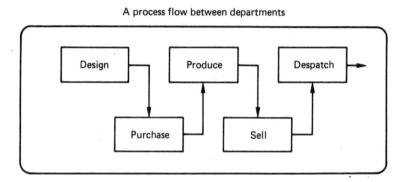

Figure 11 *All work is a process.*

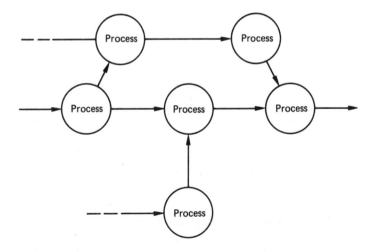

Figure 12 *The real way to understand the organisation of work.*

Supplier–Customer Relationships

In the description on page 69 the term 'final or external customer' was used. In business the term 'customer' is usually used to mean the external customer, but within the process flow each interdependent process has both customer(s) and supplier(s) who are likely to be inside the organisation. The final output of these linked processes will only delight the external customer, and do so at the lowest cost to the producer, when each individual process delights its internal customer each and every time. If a process yields output which does not meet the requirements of the next process, one of two things will happen. Either the final customer will receive defective goods or the company will be involved in expensive waste of resources through inspection, rework and material loss.

Quality starts when every individual in a company understands that he, and the process in which he is involved, are in a customer–supplier relationship (Figure 13). People may work for years in an organisation and never meet an external customer. Yet if they fail to meet the requirements of their internal customer, the company is in danger of losing the external one. The flow or chain of interconnected processes is only as strong as its weakest link.

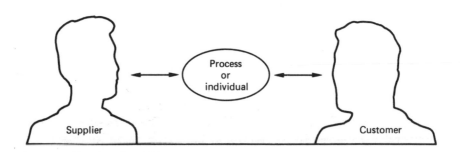

Figure 13 *Every individual and every process has a customer and a supplier. This relationship is the key to communication within the company.*

Management, People and Processes

The least understood but the most important truth about the organisation of work is that people work *in* processes and management works *on* processes. Most of the systems developed by management for the control of work not only ignore this principle but are diametrically opposed to it. Comprehension of the issue must start with an understanding of the nature of work processes. Figure 14 illustrates the requirements that are essential for a conforming controlled process.

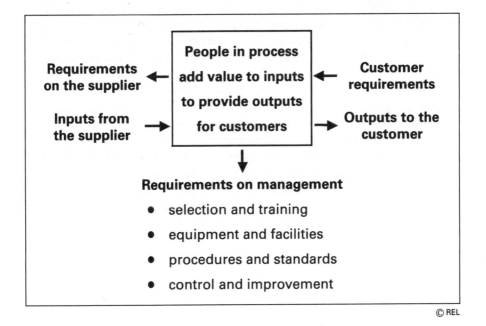

© REL

Figure 14 *Management's task is to analyse and manage processes.*

The objective of the process, whether manufacturing or administrative, is to meet the requirements of the customer. Once these have been established, the requirements can be defined for the supplier. However, this is not enough to ensure that the process consistently meets the customer's requirements. The process itself has requirements which must be met consistently. The input and output examples given earlier indicated that the process of agreeing a mortgage loan would also require standard loan rates and calculators or computer systems to allow the outputs to be produced. The diagram in Figure 14 illustrates the type of requirements essential to the process. The procedures and policies for operating the process must be defined. The equipment and facilities must be provided to enable the process to meet the customer requirements. Above all, the people working in the process must have the requisite training and skills. Unless all of these are present, the process is unlikely to always meet the customer requirements.

That's all very logical and may seem a reasonable analysis of a work process, but where is the problem? It lies in the process requirements. Only management has the power and resources to provide these requirements. Only management can see that the right equipment is available or ensure that the people working in the process have the requisite skills and training. It is also management's duty to define procedures and standards and to see that these are clearly communicated to the relevant people. Management must ensure that the process is right from the outset and is maintained in a stable and controlled manner.

More than 80 per cent of the problems that arise in industry and commerce are due to faults in the system. The statisticians call this 'common cause'. In other words, the process requirements are not being met. The wrong equipment is being used, or the right equipment has not been properly maintained. The correct procedures for operating the process were not established, or were not properly communicated. Or the people working in the process were not properly trained to carry out their actions in the process. All of these faults are the responsibility of management. However willing or dedicated, the people working in the process are powerless to change the system. They are quite likely to know what is wrong, but management do not think to ask them.

The workers are confused with unclear instructions, then become frustrated when despite their complaints management does nothing. Steadily cynicism sets in and they become 'bloody minded'. Why should they bother about quality if management clearly does not care? Managers sail blithely on without changing their ways. From time to time they will launch motivational programmes to make the workers aware of quality, or a 'drive for excellence' or even a slogan like 'our customers come first.' They then wonder why this has only a minor effect. The answer is that, quite apart from the workers' understandable cynicism, they cannot impact more than 20 per cent of the problems at the workplace without active co-operation from management. This is why quality circles are a relative failure. They will work if they are supported by managers who know that 80 per cent of the problems are the fault of management, and behave accordingly.

The present organisational structure of most companies (see Figure 15) obscures management's view of what is really happening. As the organisation is generally departmental or functionally oriented, the management focus is upon departments. Senior management rarely considers the business in terms of the multiplicity of processes involved in these departments. Control and direction of work and communication to middle management and their people is almost always vertical and departmental. The processes themselves flow horizontally and therefore demand a high level of lateral communication between departments. But instead, this management viewpoint forces the departments to operate as islands unto themselves.

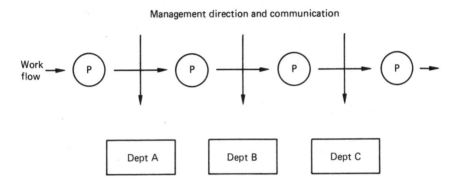

Figure 15 *Management's view of the flow of work processes is obscurred by the department organisations they establish.*

The net result of the departmental approach is illustrated in Figure 16. Not only are independent fortresses created, but the same attitude is taken by both management and people to communication within and between work processes. Effective barriers to communication are established within work processes, with little or no reference or communication to customers and suppliers. The barriers have to be removed, and this can best be achieved by a work ethos of defining and agreeing requirements with all concerned.

Management theory since the war has concentrated on the management of people rather than the management of processes. This has varied from the 'strong' management of MBO and staff appraisals to the behavioural management of transactional analysis. Middle management, rather than working with and helping their people, have become adept at implementing systems to measure people numerically. People react to MBO stimuli by meeting vertical objectives which almost force them to ignore other co-operative requirements.

Dr Deming includes 'drive out fear' as one of his fourteen points for management. Numerical measurement of people creates stress and fear. Young aspiring managers are sent to week-long seminars to measure how they stand up to stress. This is seen as the natural order of things in

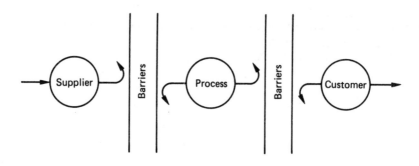

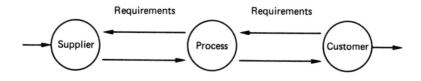

Figure 16 *The barriers to communication must be removed by defining and agreeing requirements.*

big business. Figure 17 illustrates this management obsession with measuring people. Managers think that the way to manage is to set tough goals for their people – but whenever a manager sets a goal for an employee, that worker will strive to please the boss even at the expense of the process.

In reality, management should be concentrating on releasing the potential of people. They should concentrate on *removing* fear and stress, not measuring how much stress can be endured (see Figure 18). People spend too much of their lives at work for it to be some kind of obstacle course. When all in the organisation co-operate to improve work processes and everything connected with their jobs, work can be fun. To quote Dr Deming again, there should be joy in work. It may seem idyllic but it *is* possible.

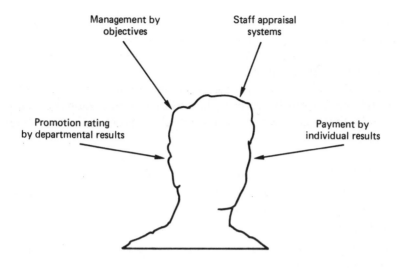

Figure 17   *Management is obsessed by the numerical measurement of people.*

The latter part of this chapter might be considered some form of motherhood by sceptical readers. The authors certainly used to believe that these were fanciful theories that had little real practical application in business life. However, in recent years we have had contact with

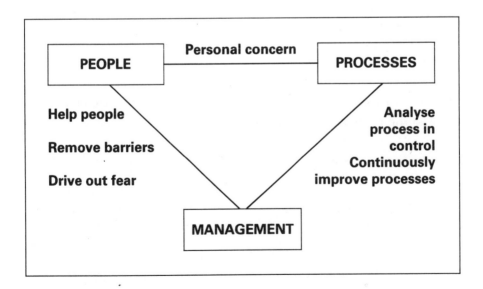

Figure 18   *The new management culture – a balanced personal concern for quality through people and processes.*

working environments that were striving to meet these ideals. It is a worthwhile objective but it is not easy; everyone at work has been conditioned over years and it is difficult to change totally. Incidentally, what is wrong with motherhood?

Readers should start by asking questions about the environment in which they are currently working. Could that environment be changed, and would that make work more enjoyable? Start with the following questions:

1 Do I always know what is expected of me?
2 Am I satisfied that I am able to do my job to the best of my ability?
3 Have I agreed the requirements of my output with my internal customer?
4 Does my manager want to know my problems in meeting the requirements of my job?
5 Do I always receive exactly what I want from my internal suppliers?
6 Have I discussed my requirements with my internal suppliers?
7 Does my company have principles and values which are understood by everyone in the organisation?
8 Can I recognise any barriers to communication in my working relationships with other departments?
9 Do my business objectives ever disagree with what seems commonsense?
10 Do I ever feel fear or stress in my job?
11 Do I know what is going on in the company, or do I feel permanently in the dark?
12 Have I asked the people reporting to me what I can do to help them?
13 Do they have any problems in meeting their job requirements?
14 List the processes you work in.

12 We cannot afford more quality

Senior management in many companies may not fully understand quality, realise who is responsible for quality or know how to manage quality. However, almost all of them do realise that the customer wants quality, and therefore they would like to achieve 'higher quality levels'. Unfortunately for them, the business schools taught them that improved quality was a trade-off with increased production costs. On this basis quality meant higher prices to the customer and thus reduced sales or margins. Initially their experience appeared to prove their tutors right, so management has attempted to find some 'optimum level of quality' which would nearly satisfy both sides of the equation. Figure 19 illustrates this typical management view of quality.

In one sense their view was right, but it was based on a false premise. They were trying to achieve a 'high level of customer satisfaction' by increasing the level of inspection and testing. The more they strove for quality, the more it cost. The high cost of quality became an ingrained truth for management. They really saw quality as a marketing issue with judgements typically expressed in statements like, 'We are not at the Rolls-Royce end of the market.' They were confusing quality with standards, or more subjectively in recent years, with excellence.

In chasing the elusive 'truth' of optimum quality, management had obscured the real truth of managing quality. They had not observed or understood that it takes time, effort and money to produce defective products. These resources are all wasted. No amount of inspection, checking or rework can ever recover the cost of this waste. Indeed, these quality activities are an additional overhead which only increases the level of wasted resources.

Production management are aware of the costs of waste and rework, but generally consider the high cost of inspection to be a necessary cost of doing business. They are unlikely to consider design and engineering rework represented by change notices or revised drawings as part of the costs of waste. Administration or marketing managers see quality and waste as concepts wholly connected with manufacturing. Yet an invoice

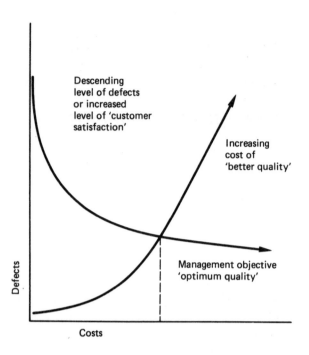

Figure 19   *Management's view of quality.*

that has to be corrected and reposted to a customer is a quality issue and is contributing to the cost of wasted resources. Equally, the time a salesman spends with a customer sorting out delivery problems or defective product is a wasted resource. Every process of work in every function of the typical company abounds with similar examples of money literally thrown away. Few managers have any real idea of how much the cumulative cost of this waste really amounts to throughout the company operations.

Businesses do in fact measure costs such as waste and rework, but usually only in the production area. Other costs such as warranty claims and premium freight may also be included. All of these examples are 'cost code items' and therefore easily recognised. But the administrative work involved in handling warranty claims in various departments is a 'hidden cost' and therefore escapes inclusion in calculations of the overall cost of quality. In a similar manner, all the wasteful work going on in administrative areas due to error, or the knock-on effect of earlier error, is hidden. These hidden and unidentified costs lead company management to believe that the total cost of quality, or more accurately the cost of *non*-quality in their operations, only represents 6 to 10 per cent of overall costs. They also tend to believe that this is normal and part of the cost of doing business. The real costs are vastly higher, and when identified usually come as a great shock to senior management.

The typical cost of waste in manufacturing industry in the West is 25 per cent of sales revenue. For every four product items produced, one is thrown away. The evidence is irrefutable. World-class companies such as IBM, 3M, Rank Xerox, Honeywell, Milliken, ICI, Philips and many other companies in the USA and Europe have all confirmed this level of waste when they commenced the drive for quality improvement. Indeed, it was the discovery of this uncomfortable fact in their individual companies that convinced them of the need to embrace total quality management.

In service industries, where nearly all these costs are of the hidden variety, the figures have to be expressed differently. Sales turnover or revenue do not have the same significance as in manufacturing, as the example of financial service companies or banks make clear. In many cases their total operating costs would be way lower than 10 per cent of turnover. However, typical costs of waste in service companies are some 30 to 40 per cent of operating costs, and in some cases the authors are aware of figures in excess of 50 per cent of operating costs.

These are horrendous costs for both manufacturing and service industries. If quality improvement could significantly reduce these costs, the need for a new commitment to quality becomes obvious. The evidence is available that they can be reduced. TQM, implemented with a constancy of purpose, will reduce these costs by as much as 75 per cent within three to four years. Many companies can provide evidence of this level of reduction in the cost of quality. Though the Japanese rarely measure the cost of quality in the same way as Western companies, general estimates indicate that comparable figures in their leading manufacturing companies would be around 5 per cent of sales revenue. It does not need a financial genius to demonstrate the massive competitive advantage this comparison provides.

There is a positive side to this negative situation. Waste at the level described provides a major opportunity, if not the best opportunity, to increase profits. A substantial proportion of the savings made by reducing waste will represent a financial contribution to the bottom line. Not all the reduction of waste can be immediately realised in cost reduction, however. For example, it may not be possible to reduce the number of employees, sell off spare space or re-organise other resources. Nevertheless, those savings that cannot be translated into immediate cost reduction are likely to provide increased capacity. The original argument for TQM was based on customer requirements. The process will reduce the cost of producing the product or service and at the same time make it more appealing to the customer. The real beauty of quality improvement as discussed in this book is that it provides an almost unbelievable win-win situation. TQM will reduce cost, improve profitability, provide more opportunities for investment and at the same time increase sales through competitive advantage.

Philip Crosby, pre-eminent in changing the thought patterns of conventional American management, expressed this concept in the title of his best-selling book, *Quality is Free*. This was a direct attack on the conventional management view that quality costs money. Eliminate waste and quality is not only free, it is a positive contribution to the cost equation. As a generalisation, every pound spent on eliminating waste can provide a saving of ten pounds. One IBM plant director is quoted as saying that the real return is nearer one hundred to one, but ten to one is pretty good odds in management decision making.

A business decision to recognise the need and commit the company to a quality improvement process is put into perspective by objectively assessing the alternatives. Many options are available to companies as they look to future growth. These could include planning a substantial increase in sales, new technology for production or a new product, an acquisition to add new products or new market areas, and many other possibilities. Any one of these approaches could be a good management decision. The common factor in each of these decision opportunities is investment and risk with no guarantee of success. For example, the decision to increase sales by a given percentage is likely to involve investment in advertising and other promotion, increasing the sales force and a new pricing structure. This investment has to be measured against the risk of failure. All the other options involve a similar investment-versus-risk decision.

The authors are not recommending businessmen to avoid investment and risk. We are saying that if the first priority was to systematically reduce the existing waste and improve quality for the customer, the risk in all the other alternatives would be reduced. The funds would be available for investment without recourse to borrowing, and the ability to satisfy the new demands of the customer and the business would be increased.

If that scenario appears all too easy, the question needs to be asked, how else have the Japanese, with no natural material resources, managed to competitively ship better-performing products around the world? Western industrialists and politicians sometimes seem to believe that Japan has achieved her penetration of Western markets by government subsidy or some skilful form of dumping. Any capitalist economist could quickly prove that such a policy would have a fairly limited life. The Japanese are by no means lily-white and can certainly employ underhand or crafty marketing ploys to protect their own markets whilst penetrating others. But a realist would have to say that they created the marketing power to make these shenanigans possible. They achieved that power by a quality revolution – a revolution that reduced the costs of manufacture while at the same time achieving totally new standards of quality.

Figure 20 illustrates the real truth of quality improvement – a simple secret that can revolutionise the opportunities for management. The authors hope that the business schools will learn the lesson so that they can help the next generations of managers.

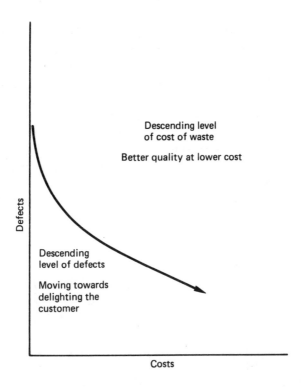

Figure 20 *The real view of quality management opportunity.*

Managers confronted for the first time with these theories, or even other companies' experience, will still doubt that the level of waste we have described really applies to their company. They have probably been successful managers in successful companies and thus their scepticism is understandable. The authors hold the view that management *should* be sceptical of the latest management theory of the too-easy leap onto the bandwagon of the guru of the day. As long as the attitude is scepticism rather than cynicism, it can provide a helpful transition to real understanding and commitment.

The starting point for the sceptic is to recognise that the claims of the argument in this chapter are so dramatic that they at least demand some investigation. In other words, it is essential to assess the level of waste in his own company. This exercise will provide a firm foundation for demonstrating the need for change in the company. For this reason, even the management team that is totally convinced by our argument should carry out an assessment of waste. The techniques for this assessment are developed in detail in Chapter 23.

The detailed assessment of waste is concerned with specific identification and costing of waste to establish a picture for the whole company. But even without undertaking this exercise the reader can begin to gain an appreciation of the level of waste in his own operation. Rather than calculating cost, it can be helpful and illuminating to consider the daily use of his time and the amount of hassle he encounters as part of his normal duties. Start with the premise that if everything in the chain of work processes throughout the organisation is done exactly right, every time, then there will be very little hassle or wasted time. How does the reader's typical day or week compare with this idyllic position?

In making an individual assessment there are several points to bear in mind. These points are helpful principles in understanding what comprises waste and how it can be recognised. The points can be summarised as follows:

1 Waste is the incurred cost of not conforming to a customer's agreed requirements (whether the customer is internal or external).
2 Waste is not necessarily found where it was originally caused.
3 Some whole processes, cost codes or functions and the people involved in them can be classified as waste.
4 Waste piles upon waste; one defect can create others, or alternatively a defect carried forward through a series of processes will compound the original waste.
5 Waste carries its own overhead, like all other activities of the organisation.

For the purpose of the individual assessment it will be worthwhile to consider items 2 and 3 more closely. The definition in item 1 relates directly to the description of work processes in the previous chapter.

In Chapter 10 an example was cited of a factory in the computer industry where 44 per cent of the sales orders received were wrong. A chain of processes were involved in this situation. These included marketing, sales, sales order processing, production planning and production. The example made clear that waste was incurred in sales, sales order processing and production planning. The most substantial costs of waste were actually incurred in production, who assembled the wrong system and were involved in substantial rework to meet the real customer requirement. Very little waste was found in the marketing operation – yet their error or non-comformance was the prime cause of the overall level of waste in the company in this particular case. Production actually caused none of the waste in this example. In some environments where the cost of quality is used as a measure, unjust comparisons can be established.

The lesson to be learned from this example is to look at processes, not people or departments. Finding the level of waste in an organisation is not a matter of finger-pointing or establishing blame. For every item of waste found in one operation which can be attributed to error in that operation, there is probably one more caused by error elsewhere. Once this concept is wholly understood, individuals or departments can begin to assess waste in an objective manner without being defensive. The hypothetical, but typical, story of a new product launch in Chapter 9 illustrated an interlocking chain of events and work processes which wholly support this lesson. Actions were taken in many separate areas, each of which created waves of error and waste spreading in a variety of directions.

We get into a particularly sensitive area in assessing waste when we realise that whole departments can be categorised as waste. A customer complaints department is an obvious example. Perhaps less obviously, the operations involved in inspection, reconciliation and warranty issues are also waste. They can be excellently managed departments, staffed with dedicated and efficient people, but their *raison d'etre* is finding error or alleviating the results of it. Rework operations in a production facility are another example of wasted resources. The problem here is compounded because not only are they wholly involved in correcting error, but by tradition only the most competent workers are allocated to rework.

Many companies see after-sales service as a positive contribution to delighting the customer. It is true that customers will rate after-sales service as a factor in their perception of the company. However, the key to assessing after-sales service when searching out waste is to analyse the nature of the work. Many products require some form of planned maintenance. Oils have to be changed, some parts for technical reasons will not have the same life as the basic product, and other parts by the nature of the product are subject to wear. In other words, a proportion of after-sales service is an essential element in doing business and can be excluded from waste calculations. But how many service calls are the result of defective work or parts? This element of customer after-sales service is in reality waste.

The authors are not suggesting that all these examples of waste can be eliminated overnight. The real purpose of measuring waste is to focus management's attention on these issues. From this viewpoint the question to be asked when assessing waste is, 'Do we really want to be involved, if we do not have to be, in this additional expenditure?' This is not to be viewed as a mere cost-cutting exercise, but as a way to plan for the future. If the company established processes which continually delighted customers, these functions would not be required. Once Japanese management decided as a long-term plan that they did not want factory inventories or massive after-sales operations, their minds were focused on how to eliminate or reduce these functions. The result was 'just-in-time' manufacturing systems and new car engine designs that extended normal service intervals from 1500 to 9000 miles. Knowledge of the sources of waste can drive innovation.

There are many other implications involved when the subject of non-conformance or waste is studied objectively and in detail. The concepts will develop as the company works seriously at eliminating error and continuously improving processes. At this stage, though, the reader should return to an assessment of his or her own involvement in the wasteful processes common to all companies. Once again, consider the typical day or week in the workplace and answer some questions:

1　Is all my time spent on planned and scheduled activities?
2　Do I always receive materials or information I need to complete my work without chasing up another department?
3　How much of my time is spent in disputes with other departments or my immediate colleagues?
4　How much of my time is spent trying to solve problems or trouble-shooting?
5　How much of my time is spent re-doing work I have previously completed?
6　How much of my time could be classified as dealing with staff grievances or customer complaints?
7　Have I consciously passed on work I knew was incorrect or not completed?

13　But our business is different

Most managers believe that their problems with quality are peculiar to their own organisation or industry. This is particularly noticeable when individual managers from manufacturing and commercial services are gathered together to discuss quality. In manufacturing, managers within the construction or process industries believe that they have little in common with production-line manufacturing. Even within the same company, managers tend to believe that their problems are unique. To them it is an obvious fact of life that the problems in the sales office are totally different from those encountered on the shop floor. Their industries or functions *are* different but the *nature* and root cause of their problems are not unique.

Teaching quality management over the years the author has invited thousands of managers to share their problems with quality. These managers have been drawn from almost every industry or functional discipline and a wide range of nationalities. Without exception, after the most perfunctory examination of the nature and cause of a problem, it was possible to categorise them under three headings: people, management and communications.

Managers do of course face technical problems, but these are rarely associated with quality. However, many quality problems are blamed on technology which in reality have nothing to do with equipment or technology. A simple example which is familiar to everyone will suffice to illustrate the point. Every customer both internal and external, when faced with faulty or dilatory service, has heard the excuse that it was due to 'a computer error'. Never accept that excuse without detailed explanation, for there is very rarely a genuine computer problem. Someone wrote the computer program, and some individual in the organisation was responsible for the input of data to the computer. Even a hardware fault is usually caused by people. To believe otherwise would be to accept that technology controls people rather than the reverse. Some novelists project this position as an awful harbinger of the future, but business is not there yet. No, technology blinds people to the reality of a situation or is used as a convenient crutch. Too many customers, who feel uncomfortable with modern business technology, are prepared to accept that this is the way things are done and leave befuddled, lamenting the passing of the old ways. The business carries on as usual with no imperative to change and face up to its shortcomings.

Whatever the industry or service, there are three personnel groups which always seem to have difficulty in associating their special functions with the total quality management process. They all seem to believe that the very nature of their jobs puts them outside the normal management disciplines or any form of process analysis. These groups can be broadly categorised as (1) the sales force, (2) the specialists, including designers, software developers and lawyers, and (3) research and development.

All of these groups see themselves as having unique, highly specialised and individual skills which they lend to the company for a commission or salary. They tend to view management as an unnecessary intrusion into their creative role and special status. They see themselves as individuals having rare creative skills to whom the normal rules do not apply. They often dress differently in a subconscious proclamation of their independence of the surrounding 'company politics'. In their view management do not understand the peculiar pressures on creative people and are always making unreasonable demands. They are partially justified in that view but they also misunderstand their role in the overall process.

Before continuing, the author hastens to add that he is not exhibiting a management prejudice towards the creative functions. He actually started his career in architecture, founded a predominantly software-based computer service company for the construction industry in the fifties, and has been both a salesman and a manager of substantial sales forces. However, he does plead ignorance of the law.

Concepts like 'right first time' or 'zero defects' are anathema to the creative specialists. The designer believes that it is impossible to design a new car right first time. The industrial chemist in research and development knows that he cannot develop a new drug right first time. No modern invention was created absolutely right first time. These are all iterative processes with a great deal of associated trial and error. However, they are processes surrounded by a host of other processes which must be in control if the research is to be successful. Every stage must be properly recorded and measured so that old avenues can be re-opened as another direction is aborted. Measuring devices must be accurately calibrated and constant environments maintained. In fact everything that has been said in this book about quality management not only applies to design, research and development but can be a positive aid to the creative specialist.

There is a perennial debate about whether salesmen are born or made. In the authors' experience there are individuals who have innate skills which particularly suit them to selling. But that is true of many vocations. The selling process is itself a series of interconnected processes. Almost without exception (excluding special relationships or bribery) a post-mortem on a lost sale will unearth a sub-process that was omitted or improperly conducted. Companies build a mystique around salesmanship and encourage selfish individualism by their reward structure and numerical objectives. They can pay a heavy price for this managerial approach in future relations with the customer and in the impact on all the supporting functions and processes. More than any other kind of employee in the company, the salesman is only as good as his last month's figures. This pressure does not encourage co-operation with other departments or interest in the wider aspects of the business.

Another area surrounded by mystique is that of software design. It is considered axiomatic that all computer programs will contain bugs, as it is impossible to develop a thousand lines of code without error. Bugs in software are errors and not part of the iterative creative process. System design is creative but program coding is not. Mistakes may be made, as they will in any process, but they should never be accepted as a necessary evil of the process. Computer programming is based on carefully designed and defined systemic rules. If they are consistently followed, bug-free programs should be produced as output of the process. Errors can be caused by faults in the design of the coding system as well as by individual inattention to the rules. However, if error is accepted as a natural part of the process there will be no inducement to seek or detect the root cause of a particular error. The same mistake will be repeated over and over again. In many cases this is cited as evidence to prove the point that bugs are endemic to software production.

The growing importance of the skilled specialist or knowledge worker is an inescapable fact of modern business. To some extent this fact has helped to foster the myths that surround these activities. But his dependence on specialist functions indicates how vital it is to the health of a business that these functions are successfully involved in the process of continuous improvement. The difficulty of convincing the specialist that they are part of an interdependent process network must not be an excuse to allow the perpetuation of independent functional fortresses. These operations will not recognise the need to change – a problem of communication and education that will be addressed in Chapter 28.

All industries, all functions and all companies *are* different. They differ in operational methods, in attitudes and in a host of cultural aspects. Knowledge of these differences is an essential element in planning awareness, education and other communications within a company. However, the concepts that have been discussed in earlier chapters apply equally to all these disparate entities. Chapter 11 highlighted the cultural factors that lie behind all work processes. It was clearly demonstrated that defects or error always have their root cause in the attitudes of people, the behaviour of management or the communications between interdependent people and processes.

If you still have any doubts that the quality-management principles presented in the book really apply to your own company, or your particular function within it, ask yourself the following questions:

1   Identify specialist activities in the company. Do the specialist employees exhibit different attitudes from those of other employees?
2   If so, what are some of the differences?
3   How many quality problems can you identify that do not have their roots in people, communications or management?

PART TWO

The Principles of Quality Management

*What the experts – the gurus – have to
say about quality management. Which
approach will fit your company.*

14 Which guru to follow?

A multitude of consultants offer solutions to the problems of achieving quality improvement. Most of these solutions are based on the teachings of three American experts on quality who have become known as 'the gurus' – Philip Crosby, Dr W. Edwards Deming and Dr Joseph Juran.

A number of other experts have contributed to the recent evolution of quality management without quite reaching the pre-eminence of the three gurus. Most notable among these is Armand Feigenbaum, who was the first to start using the word 'total' in relation to quality. Though the Japanese quality revolution was originally based on the work of Deming and Juran, the Japanese are, as might be expected, adding their own experts who are influencing thought in this area. These include Profesor Kaori Ishikawa, Genichi Taguchi, Musaaki Imai and Shiguru Mizuno.

Executives considering quality improvement can be confused as to which expert or guru to follow. This confusion is natural because each guru is promoted by some of his followers as the sole fount of all wisdom. The gurus themselves sometimes do not appear to have much time for each other, but in fairness the conflict is more often the fault of their protagonists rather than the gurus themselves.

Confused company managers are faced with a plethora of jargon and slogans. 'Absolutes', 'steps', 'points', statistics and project-oriented groups are all paraded as the necessary elements of quality improvement. In truth there is more that unites than divides in the teaching of the gurus. They all preach that management commitment and involvement are the key to quality improvement. Each, in his own way, emphasises that the attitude of workers to quality will change only when management behaviour changes. All agree that technology alone plays little part in quality improvement and have little time for quality circles, the favourite device of 'quick fix' management advocates.

An article by Jeremy Main in *Fortune* magazine in August 1986, entitled 'Under the Spell of the Gurus', illustrated the popular, somewhat naive viewpoint of the differences between the experts when he posed the

question, 'Which guru should your company choose?' and then
continued, 'The menu of possibilities is wildly varied, with offerings that
range from the bland to the incendiary. Do you want an inspirational
type like Phil Crosby, who will send the corporate staff charging up the
hill under a banner inscribed Zero Defects? Or do you want a technical
type . . . who will work quietly alongside your engineers? Perhaps you
masochistically crave fiery denunciations from the 85-year-old W.
Edwards Deming, who will probably tell your managers they are a pack
of idiots.'

Both of the authors have worked with the concepts of several different
gurus over a number of years. We have never believed that one expert
has a monopoly of all wisdom on the subject of quality. Quality
management is not a fixed body of revealed truths but a *process* that is
evolving and will take on differing forms to meet the needs of individual
companies. Corporations faithful to any of the three gurus have
transformed their performance and become quality leaders in their own
markets. Other large corporations in both the USA and the UK have
intentionally utilised the advice of *all* the gurus, as well as other experts,
with considerable success. Although the teachings of the various experts
differ in content and emphasis, each has wisdom that can be included in
every company's total quality management process.

IBM, one of the earliest major Western companies to commit itself to
quality, made a deliberate policy of working with a number of quality
consultants. Senior management attended classes on quality management led by Crosby, Juran and Deming. Other consultants, such as
Feigenbaum, were involved at specific locations. Though Crosby had the
major influence on general management in the early eighties, IBM gradually developed a quality management approach which was unique to
themselves. They have been able to weld the concepts of the gurus with
their own contributions to the evolution of TQM. In Britain parts of ICI
have successfully taken a similar approach. Both companies have
created quality management processes that are distinctively their own.
Both openly recognise the contributions of the respective gurus and
consultants, but neither company attempted to develop a porridge of the
differing methods and concepts without in-depth experience of each.
The applicability of the different approaches is dependent on the culture
and nature of a business judged on a national or locational basis. The
final determinant is often only a matter of timing.

There is one discernible trend in the applicability and use of the gurus
by Western companies over the last decade. The Crosby approach has
more often been used to initiate the process of quality improvement. His
concepts and methodology are clear and easy to communicate and
therefore appeal to executives. Philip Crosby is a prolific author and
broadcaster on the subject of quality, which brings him to the attention of

senior management. In many cases his books or videos are their first contact with the concepts of quality management. In addition his thoroughly trained (opponents use the word programmed) associates are readily available through an international network of 'Quality Colleges'. Many companies that started implementing the Crosby approach are now heavily involved in the Deming approach or use Juran methodology in specific locations.

It should be noted that few, if any, of these companies now decry Crosby. Indeed, most believe that they would not have been able to start the process of change without the inspiration of his evangelism. Their awareness of the issues and the change in attitude of their employees has simply developed far enough so that they can readily use the more sophisticated approaches of the other gurus.

TQM is a process and not a one-off programme. It is therefore evolutionary in its implementation within an individual company as much as in an overall historic sense. As the process evolves in the organisation, the ideas of the gurus and other experienced implementers will all have their applicability. Every company should be aware of, and be open to, the diversity and commonality of the concepts so that they are best prepared to apply them at the right time and in the right circumstances.

The one truth that emerges from studying the gurus is that each organisation must, in effect, *take ownership* of its own quality improvement process. Whether influenced by one or a multiplicity of outside consultants, they are managing their own businesses. To achieve a sustained competitive advantage their business operations and their continuous improvement process must be indivisible.

According to one definition, a guru is the leader or chief theoretician of a movement. The drive for quality can be seen as a movement, so perhaps the term guru is appropriate. However, there is a tendency to invest them with an aura of profound knowledge and as a result to follow their concepts and methodology with blind faith. Some healthy scepticism is not out of place. Their pronouncements and teaching should provoke thought rather than be accepted as a panacea.

In reality the concepts of the gurus are not revolutionary or even particularly new. They represent a return to basic common sense in the management of organisations. Their contribution has been to refocus the eyes of management and light up areas that had become hidden. A twenty-five-year-old British Productivity Association film, *Right First Time*, described most of the concepts in a practical way. Artistically the film is dated, but the key issues are all there. Perhaps of more interest is that the principal advisors to the film makers were a firm established long before the gurus – Marks & Spencer.

15 Not by systems alone!

Many companies are or will be under pressure from their customers to show proof that they have implemented management systems complying with one or other of the current quality assurance standards or certification schemes. This approach is now international, as the International Standards Organisation chart (see Figure 21) illustrates. In the UK, accreditation to the British Standard for Quality Management (BS 5750) also satisfies the International and European Community Standards, ISO 9000 and EN 29000 respectively.

Standards body (country)	Quality management and quality assurance standards: Guidelines for selection and use	Quality systems: Model for quality assurance in design/ development, production, installation and servicing	Quality systems: Model for quality assurance in production and installation	Quality systems: Model for quality assurance in final inspection and test	Quality management and quality system elements: Guidelines
ISO	ISO 9000: 1987	ISO 9001: 1987	ISO 9002: 1987	ISO 9003: 1987	ISO 9004: 1987
Australia	AS 3900	AS 3901	AS 3902	AS 3903	AS 3904
Austria	ö Norm ISO 9000	ö Norm ISO 9001	ö Norm ISO 9002	ö Norm ISO 9003	ö Norm ISO 9004
Belgium	NBN X 50–002–1	NBN X 50–003	NBN X 50–004	NBN X 50–005	NBN X 50–002–2
Canada	CSA Z2990–86	CSA Z299.1–85	CSA Z299.2–85	CSA Z299.4–85	CSA Q420–87
Denmark	DS/ISO 9000 DS/EN 29000	DS/ISO 9001 DS/EN 29002	DS/ISO 9002 DS/EN 29002	DS/ISO 9003 DS/EN 29003	DS/ISO 9004 DS/EB 29004
Finland	SFS-ISO 9000	SFS-ISO 9001	SFS-ISO 9002	SFS-ISO 9003	SFS-ISO 9004
France	NF X 50–121	NF X 50–131	NF X 50–132	NF X 50–133	NF X 50–122
Germany (FR)	DIN ISO 9000	DIN ISO 9001	DIN ISO 9002	DIN ISO 9003	DIN ISO 9004
India	IS: 10201 Part 2	IS: 10201 Part 4	IS: 10201 Part 5	IS: 10201 Part 6	IS: 10201 Part 3
Ireland	IS 300 Part 0/ ISO 9000	IS 300 Part 1/ ISO 9001	IS 300 Part 2/ ISO 9002	IS 300 Part 3/ ISO 9003	IS 300 Part 0/ ISO 9004
Netherlands	NEN-ISO 9000	NEN-ISO 9001	NEN-ISO 9002	NEN-ISO 9003	–
Norway	–	NS 5801	NS 5802	NS 5803	
South Africa	SABS 0157: Part 0	SABS 0157: Part I	SABS 0157: Part II	SABS 0157: Part III	SABS 0157: Part IV
Spain	UNE 66 900	UNE 66 901	UNE 66 902	UNE 66 903	UNE 66 904
Switzerland	SN-ISO 9000	SN-ISO 9001	SN-ISO 9002	SN-ISO 9003	SN-ISO 9004
United Kingdom	BS 5750: 1987: Part 0: Section 0.1 ISO 9000/ EN 29000	BS 5750: 1987: Part 1: ISO 9001/ EN 29001	BS 5750: 1987: Part 2: ISO 9002/ EN 29002	BS 5750: 1987: Part 3: ISO 9003/ EN 29003	BS 5750: 1987: Part 0: Section 0.2 ISO 9004/ EN 29003
USA	ANSI/ASQC Q90	ANSI/ASQC Q91	ANSI/ASQC Q92	ANSI/ASQC Q93	ANSI/ASQC Q94
Yugoslavia	JUS A.K 1.010	JUS A.K 1.012	JUS A.K 1.013	JUS A.K 1.014	JUS A.K 1.011
European Community	EN 29000	EN 29001	EN 29002	EN 29003	EN 29004

Figure 21 *International quality standards.*

The objective of these standards is to ensure that customers receive the product or service they require, to the standards they require, every time. The standards define a logical framework that, applied correctly, will provide customer satisfaction. Companies may require certification to BS 5750 to meet marketing requirements, but they should not be under the illusion that they now have quality. Standards systems are only one part of cost-effective total quality management. Implementation of these systems will not change management behaviour or employee attitudes to the extent that is required to achieve a sustained competitive advantage.

BS 5750/ISO 9000

BS 5750 is the UK national standard for quality systems which is identical to the international standard ISO 9000. It tells suppliers and manufacturers what is required of a quality-oriented system. It does not set out special requirements which only a very few firms can comply with, but is a practical standard for quality systems which can be used by all UK industry.

The principles of BS 5750 are applicable whether the company employs ten people or ten thousand. It identifies the basic disciplines and specifies in detail the matters which should be covered in procedures to ensure that products meet the customers' requirements. BS 5750 defines quality as fitness for purpose and could be said to fall short of the TQM objective of delighting the customer, but it sets out how to establish, document and maintain an effective quality system. It is a nationally accepted standard and is simply common sense set down on paper in an organised way. It has been broken down into nineteen sections to enable manufacturers to implement it easily and efficiently.

A more detailed description of BS 5750 can be obtained from the Certification and Assessment Department, British Standards Institution, Marylands Avenue, Hemel Hempstead, Herts HP2 4SQ.

Assessment and Certification

Before applying for certification that a company complies with BS 5750 it will be necessary to carry out a survey to establish where the company stands and what more may be required. There are a large number of consultants who are qualified to do this assessment and assist companies in preparing for certification. Some of these consultants have themselves been registered as capable of carrying out assessments on behalf of certification bodies.

PERA (Production Engineering and Research Association) operates the Quality Assurance Scheme for the Department of Trade and Industry and maintains a list of qualified consultants. They can also advise on Department of Trade and Industry grants for small companies for assistance in assessment and certification. For further information write to: PERA, The Quality and Assurance Advisory Service, Melton Mowbray, Leicestershire LE13 0PB.

The consultant's survey report is likely to recommend a number of actions that are required to implement systems in preparation for certification. The company can generally rely on the consultant's report and use him to advise on the implementation of the recommendations. The time required and the level of cost involved will depend on the assessment, the type of business and the size of the company.

The survey report probably will identify areas where training is needed for supervisors and the workforce. The consultant may not be able to provide this training, but the Institute of Quality Assurance maintains a Directory of Quality Assurance Education and Training Facilities in the UK for the Department of Trade and Industry. Full details of these syllabuses can be obtained from the National Quality Information Centre at the Institute of Quality Assurance, 10 Grosvenor Gardens, London SW1W 0DQ.

The Department of Trade and Industry

The DTI has actively promoted quality improvement and assisted companies in achieving it through a series of programmes since 1983. These have included the National Quality Campaign (now included in the 'Management into the 90s' programme), and the Enterprise Initiative. The DTI provides extensive advisory and support services both nationally and regionally. An independent firm or group with a payroll of fewer than 500 can obtain financial assistance covering five to fifteen man-days of specialist consultancy support in a number of key management functions, including quality. To date this has been particularly directed at assessment for, and implementation of systems for, BS 5750 certification and since June 1989 has included TQM.

The Secretary of State for Trade and Industry accredits certification bodies which he considers meet approved standards of competence, integrity and impartiality. He is advised by the National Accreditation Council for Certification Bodies (NACCB).

The DTI also produces or makes available a large number of publications and videos on the whole subject of quality, from the techniques of metrology to the concepts of the quality management gurus. They can be contacted through more than a dozen regional offices, but full information can be obtained through their central office.

16 The evangelist

Philip B. Crosby has done more to wake up Western management to the need for quality improvement, and their responsibility for it, than all the other gurus and experts combined. Starting with *Quality is Free* a series of his books, speeches and broadcasts have influenced thousands of executives to change their behaviour and commit themselves to quality. It is worth noting that the majority of the major Western firms that have become world-class quality companies started their own internal quality revolutions with Crosby.

His critics (and there are many) refer to him as a 'mere evangelist' with little real substance. Crosby is certainly an evangelist, but why should that be considered a negative attribute? Few total conversions are achieved in the minds of men (or women) without an element of emotion and evangelism. To say that the Crosby approach has *no* substance is palpable nonsense. His systems and detailed methodology have made a major contribution to many leading and sophisticated companies. However, if the extremes are eliminated there are some germs of truth in the more general criticisms.

Two articles in *Fortune* magazine gave voice to criticism from Crosby's principal competitors in the USA, Juran and the disciples of Deming. In an article by Jaclyn Fierman in the April 1985 issue, Crosby acknowledged that 'Deming and I are on differing planets', and in the same article David Garvin, an associate professor at Harvard Business School, is quoted as saying, 'As a program for changing attitudes [Crosby's] course makes good sense . . . as a basis for specific action, it's seriously lacking.' In the August 1986 issue author Jeremy Main quotes Juran as stating, 'I do not regard Crosby as an expert in the field of quality . . . he is an expert in public relations. He is a combination of P. T. Barnum and Pied Piper.'

Crosby's best-known slogan is the exhortation to achieve 'zero defects'. Juran and Deming would argue that it is pointless, if not hypocritical, to exhort a worker on the line to turn out a perfect product when the overwhelming majority of imperfections are due to poorly designed manufacturing systems that workers cannot change. Some of this criticism has the smell of sour grapes, and the last criticism is a travesty of what Crosby actually teaches on the subject of zero defects. Crosby maintains that he does teach the tools of improvement, but even his admirers agree that he is more inspirational than practical.

In view of the claims that Crosby's approach lacks practicality, it should be noted that Philip Crosby has considerably more practical experience of managing quality from the factory floor upwards than either of his main critics. He began his career in quality as an inspector on the factory floor. It was as quality manager of the Pershing missile programme at Martin Marietta that he espoused the zero defects standard which became a key element of his teachings. There is some argument as to who originally conceived zero defects as a concept. This is now generally believed to be James Halpin at Martin Marietta, who wrote a book on the subject published by McGraw-Hill in 1964. However, Crosby did become its principal exponent in later years.

Crosby later became Vice President of Quality at ITT, where he convinced Harold Geneen to resource a cultural revolution. The 'elevator speech' Crosby used to convince Geneen is now included in Crosby courses. Crosby established an organisation in the vast ITT empire that became the model for his Fourteen Steps methodology. With the publication of *Quality is Free*, Crosby left ITT to start his own company, Philip Crosby Associates (PCA). He built PCA into a worldwide company with 'Quality Colleges' in the main centres all teaching exactly the same courses. In early 1989 PCA was sold to the Proudfoot Organisation, but Philip Crosby still advises the organisation.

The essence of what Crosby teaches is contained in what he calls the 'Four Absolutes of Quality' and in a fourteen-step process of quality improvement. His various books and other contributions to thought in this area not only develop these concepts but add perceptions on the way management should behave that are not unlike two of Deming's Fourteen Points, 'drive out fear' and 'remove the barriers to communication'. Though not included in the kernel of his concepts, his continual admonition that the job of management is 'to help people' is at the heart of the TQM movement. Crosby argues that to manage quality you must have:

- a *definition* for quality that can be readily understood by all. The start of a common language that will aid communication.
- a *system* by which to manage quality.
- a *performance standard* that leaves no room for doubt or fudging by any employee.
- a *method of measurement* which will focus attention on the progress of quality improvement.

This is all eminently sensible and provides the premise for Crosby's 'Four Absolutes' for managing quality:

1 The definition   Quality is conformance to requirements, not goodness.

2 The system   Prevention, not appraisal.

3 The performance standard   Zero defects; not 'that's close enough'.

4 The measurement   The price of non-conformance to requirements (Cost of Quality), not quality indices.

Apart from the term 'Absolute', which smacks of divine inspiration (or at the very least inspiration from Plato rather than Aristotle), these have proved acceptable principles for a large number of companies. Disciples of Deming argue that these principles ignore the concept of continuous improvement, or the constant reduction of process variation. Crosby adherents say that continuous improvement is a requirement that must be established by management and that the performance standard would involve all employees in continually improving work processes. The authors themselves now have some disagreements with the first and fourth Absolutes, but none of this really matters. The point is that these principles have proved easy to communicate and have had a real impact on changing attitudes to quality. None of the statisticians have been able to encapsulate their concepts in such a readily understood manner.

The Crosby methodology for implementation is contained within the fourteen-step quality improvement process. This process is clearly based on his experience in implementing quality improvement through the multi-disciplined ITT environment in the seventies. These steps have proved successful in many companies and therefore demand careful examination before a too-sceptical rejection. However, they are at the root of many of the critisicms of Crosby as having little practical application.

CROSBY'S FOURTEEN STEPS

as defined in the Philips company publication
Three of a Kind

1 Management Commitment
   Purpose: To make it clear where management stands on quality.
2 The Quality Improvement Team
   Purpose: To run the quality improvement programme.

3 Quality Measurement
Purpose: To provide a display of current and potential non-conformance problems in a manner that permits objective evaluation and corrective action.

4 The Cost of Quality
Purpose: To define the ingredients of the cost of quality, and explain its use as a management tool.

5 Quality Awareness
Purpose: To provide a method of raising the personal concern felt by all personnel in the company toward the conformance of the product or service and the quality reputation of the company.

6 Corrective Action
Purpose: To provide a systematic method of resolving for ever the problems that are identified through previous action steps.

7 Zero Defects Planning
Purpose: To examine the various activities that must be conducted in preparation for formally launching the Zero Defects program.

8 Supervisor Training
Purpose: To define the type of training that supervisors need in order actively to carry out their part of the quality improvement programme.

9 ZD Day
Purpose: To create an event that will let all employees realise, through a personal experience, that there has been a change.

10 Goal Setting
Purpose: To turn pledges and commitments into action by encouraging individuals to establish improvement goals for themselves and their groups.

11 Error-Cause Removal
Purpose: To give the individual employee a method of communicating to management the situations that make it difficult for the employee to meet the pledge to improve.

12 Recognition
Purpose: To appreciate those who participate.

13 Quality Councils
Purpose: To bring together the professional quality people for planned communication on a regular basis.

14 Do It Over Again
Purpose: To emphasise that the quality improvement programme never ends.

The fourteen steps do not fit all national or even company cultures. If treated as guidelines to be considered in implementing quality improvement, they are effective. Unfortunately, many Crosby adherents and even Crosby Associates teachers tend to promote them on the same level as the Absolutes. The concept of Zero Defects Day (Step 9) does have considerable relevance in involving people in the process, but can be easily misunderstood in a multi-cultural environment. Perhaps the strongest criticism is that these implementation steps give little emphasis to the management of work processes. In fairness to Crosby, the PCA internal education system does give substantial emphasis to this approach, so it could be claimed that it is contained in Supervisor Training (Step 8). The implementation of TQM must be designed to fit the nature of the business and the culture of the company; the fourteen-step process can be too rigorous or inflexible to meet this objective.

Philip Crosby has built a substantial worldwide organisation. PCA offices and their concomitant Quality Colleges are spread regionally across America and Europe and are also represented in Southeast Asia. Fundamentally his services are based on educational courses, though consultant services are available.

Deming and Juran are rightfully acknowledged as the fathers of the Japanese revolution. However, it is not generally recognised that Crosby concepts are taught under licence by the Japan Management Association to the host of smaller Japanese companies trying to emulate their bigger brothers.

17 The statistician

Dr W. Edwards Deming is generally considered the father of the Japanese quality revolution, and an American minor guru, William E. Conway, described him as 'father of the third wave of the industrial revolution'. Initially largely ignored in the United States, Dr Deming became a prophet in his own land when NBC-TV produced a documentary in June 1980 entitled *If Japan Can, Why Can't We?* NBC gave him much of the credit for the economic miracle in Japan.

Deming has certainly had a major influence on the Japanese, starting when the Union of Japanese Scientists and Engineers (JUSE) invited him to address them in June 1950. This was followed by a meeting with the presidents of twenty-one major Japanese companies, including the present-day world giants Sony, Nissan, Mitsubishi and Toyota. The Deming Prize for Quality is still eagerly sought by leading Japanese companies.

To consider him the sole instigator of the Japanese conversion, however, is perhaps to stretch a point and ignores the influence of Dr Juran. Nor can the incredible achievements of the American Government of Japan under the control of the USA's first and last pro-consul, General MacArthur, be pushed aside. It was this government that invited Deming to Japan in 1947 to help prepare for the 1951 Japanese Census. This call for Dr Deming's help recognised his activities in revolutionising the decennial United States Census in 1940. The work of the TWI (Training Within Industries) agency of MacArthur's government contributed greatly to Japanese industrial interest in quality as early as 1949 and had much to do with creating the environment in which interest was provoked in the work of Deming and Juran.

Deming's message to the Japanese was really quite simple. It is contained in his famous 'Chain Reaction' (see Figure 22). Like most messages which go to the heart of an issue, Deming's ideas appeared so simple that at first they were largely ignored or acted as profound knowledge only to those who seek knowledge and act upon it. They were at the root of Ishikawa's definition of quality management noted in

Chapter 1. At that time (and to a great extent today) Deming's approach appeared as the complete antithesis of conventional management thinking. Once his new approach was accepted, Deming could concentrate on showing the Japanese how to improve quality by the use of the statistical control of processes.

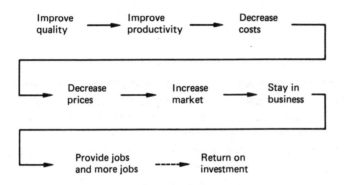

Figure 22 *Deming's chain reaction.*

Since 1980 Deming's influence on Western thinking has grown rapidly. He is an exceptionally energetic nonagenarian (he was born in 1900) who consults and travels the world to lead his famous four-day seminars. His disciples now abound, and there are Deming groups dedicated to promoting his teachings in many countries. Unlike Crosby, and to a lesser extent Juran, he has not formed a worldwide organisation of colleges or licensed consultants. At one stage there was an eager group of statisticians known as the Cosmo Club (from their meeting place) who learnt at Dr Deming's feet. This group has grown and they are often referred to today as the 'Deming Masters'. Most retain close contact with Deming and act as consultants teaching the Deming method.

Europe as well as the USA has thriving Deming groups who hold seminars often attended by as many as four to five hundred leaders of industry. Some come away bemused. Most Western managers are not statistically numerate. One could bemoan the fact, but that is not the point. If they are to change, they need more than statistical theory to provide the spark. Interestingly, Deming now spends much more time expounding his management philosophy contained in his Fourteen Points for Management. His influence in the West has accelerated since that change in approach.

The main thrust of Philip Crosby's approach is to eliminate error. Deming goes far beyond this goal. The main thrust of his philosophy is the planned reduction of variation. Productivity improves as variability decreases. Since all things vary, he says, we need to use statistical methods to control work processes 'Statistical control does not imply absence of defective items. It is a state of random variation, in which the limits of variation are predictable,' he says.

Deming is also strongly against motivational programmes which have little lasting effect and misunderstand the role of the worker. 'How can a man do it right first time when the incoming material is off gauge, off colour, or otherwise defective, or if his machine is not in good order?' This is sometimes taken as an attack on Crosby, but it is actually directed against the misuse of zero defects as a motivational tool in the United States during the sixties. Crosby does not use zero defects as a motivational device, indeed he expressly warns against the practice. He defines it as a standard which will force error to be investigated rather than ignored.

Deming's views on the role of management and a participating workforce are all contained in his constantly repeated Fourteen Points. Dr Henry Neave, Director of Research for the British Deming Association, in a pamphlet on the Deming philosophy issued by the Department of Trade and Industry, presented Deming's Fourteen Points (listed below) with this warning: 'They are not written in tablets of stone: indeed he still frequently makes minor adjustments to some of them, reflecting the way that he sees the world changing and the changing needs of the people with whom he works.'

DEMING'S FOURTEEN POINTS

1   Constancy of Purpose

Create constancy of purpose for continual improvement of products and service . . . allocating resources to provide for long-range needs rather than short-term profitability, with a plan to become competitive, to stay in business, and to provide jobs.

2   The New Philosophy

Adopt the new philosophy. We are in a new economic age, created in Japan. . . . We can no longer live with commonly-accepted levels of delays, mistakes, defective materials and defective workmanship. Transformation of Western management style is necessary to halt the continued decline in industry.

3   Cease Dependence on Inspection

Eliminate the need for mass inspection as a way to achieve quality

. . . by building quality into the product in the first place. Require statistical evidence of built-in quality in both manufacturing and purchasing functions.

4   End 'Lowest Tender' Contracts

End the practice of awarding business solely on the basis of price tag. . . . Instead, require meaningful measures of quality along with price. Reduce the number of suppliers for the same item by eliminating those that do not qualify with statistical evidence of quality. The aim is to minimise total cost, not merely initial cost. Purchasing managers have a new job, and must learn it.

5   Improve Every Process

Improve constantly and forever every process for planning, production and service. . . . Search continually for problems in order to improve every activity in the company, to improve quality and productivity and thus to constantly decrease costs. It is the management's job to work continually on the system (design, incoming materials, maintenance, improvement of machines, training, supervision, retraining).

6   Institute Training on the Job

Institute modern methods of training on the job . . . including management, to make better use of all employees. New skills are required to keep up with changes in materials, methods, product design, machinery, techniques and service.

7   Institute Leadership

Adopt and institute leadership aimed at helping people to do a better job. . . . The responsibility of managers and supervisors must be changed from sheer numbers to quality. Improvement of quality will automatically improve productivity. Management must ensure that immediate action is taken on reports of inherited defects, maintenance requirements, poor tools, fuzzy operational definitions and other conditions detrimental to quality.

8   Drive out Fear

Encourage effective two-way communication and other means to drive out fear throughout the organisation . . . so that everybody may work effectively and more productively for the company.

9   Break Down Barriers

Break down barriers between departments and staff areas. . . . People in different areas such as research, design, sales, administration and production must work in teams to tackle problems that may be encountered with products or service.

10   Eliminate Exhortations

Eliminate the use of slogans, posters and exhortations . . . for the workforce, demanding zero defects and new levels of productivity, without providing methods. Such exhortations only create adversarial relationships; the bulk of the causes of low quality and low productivity belong to the system and thus lie beyond the power of the workforce.

11   Eliminate Arbitrary Numerical Targets

Eliminate work standards that prescribe numerical quotas for the workforce and numerical goals for people in management. . . . Substitute aids and helpful supervision; use statistical methods for continual improvement of quality and productivity.

12   Permit Pride of Workmanship

Remove the barriers that rob hourly workers, and people in management, of their right to pride of workmanship. . . . This implies, inter alia, abolition of the annual merit rating (appraisal of performance) and of management by objective. Again, the responsibility of managers, supervisors, foremen must be changed from sheer numbers to quality.

13   Encourage Education

Institute a vigorous programme of education, and encourage self-improvement for everyone. . . . What an organisation needs is not just good people; it needs people that are improving with education. Advances in competitive position will have their roots in knowledge.

14   Top Management's Commitment

Clearly define top management's permanent commitment to ever-improving quality and productivity . . . and its obligation to implement all of these principles. Create a structure in top management that will push every day on the preceding 13 Points, and take action in order to accomplish the transformation.

Clearly, Deming is not just teaching statistics in his Fourteen Points, he is proclaiming a management philosophy. However, this philosophy is not acceptable to all. Dr Juran, for example, is reported as feeling that Deming is still basically a statistician who is a little out of his depth when he talks about management. Juran, and many others, believe that fear can bring out the best in people. The authors are at one with the purport of Deming's 'drive out fear', though we have some sympathy with Juran. We have also been amused at the fear Deming himself sometimes creates when he berates managers who ask what he considers a silly question!

To ignore Deming's Fourteen Points would be foolhardy in the extreme. They are too stimulating ever to be ignored.

18   The other samurai

Dr Joseph M. Juran is another active nonagenarian from the United States. His influence on the Japanese is close to that of Deming, but since the NBC TV programme mentioned in the last chapter it is not so widely recognised in the West. The Japanese recognised Dr Juran's contribution when, in 1981, Emperor Hirohito awarded him the prestigious Order of the Sacred Treasure.

The first book about management and quality read by the author (then a humble marketing director) was Juran's *Managerial Breakthroughs*. This was in 1979, and he remembers his reaction then that the book was difficult reading but intellectually stimulating. He had a similar reaction to his introduction to Deming. Though both were stimulating, they did not at that stage move the author to action. However, Crosby's book *Quality is Free* struck an immediate chord and did lead to action, though the content could hardly be called intellectual. There appears to be an awareness threshold that must be crossed before Deming's teachings, and perhaps Juran's even more so, can be appreciated. This of course is only one individual's experience, but from observation it appears that many other business managers have had similar experiences. It also explains why so many companies start with Crosby and appear to graduate to either Deming or Juran.

This view is particularly apposite to Dr Juran, because his communication style can be considered tedious to general management. His analytical approach, dotting every 'i' and crossing every 't', appeals to the engineer and the project-oriented manager. He is thorough and meticulous, in fact the very essence of quality, but not always designed to grab attention. As an indication, the latest edition of the *Quality Control Handbook*, edited by Juran, can be weighed in pounds rather than counted in pages. This is perhaps a pity, because Juran's contribution to quality thinking is without parallel.

As long ago as the 1940s Juran was highlighting managerial responsibility for quality and emphasising that quality was achieved through people rather than techniques. Though a statistician himself, he pointed out that companies could know all about the technical aspects of quality, such as statistical process control, but this did not help them to *manage* quality. He was the first of the gurus to work out that achieving quality was all about communication, management and people.

Juran details three basic steps to quality improvement: structured annual improvement plans, massive training programmes involving the whole workforce, and senior management leadership. He is at one with Deming in maintaining that the majority of quality problems are systemic and therefore the responsibility of management. They differ on the exact proportions but that hardly matters; the principle is the same. Juran stated that just as all managers need some training in finance, all should have training in quality so that they can participate in and manage quality improvement projects. At the same time he pointed out that senior management *must* be involved because 'all major quality problems are interdepartmental.' He added that 'pursuing departmental goals can sometimes undermine a company's overall quality mission'. The whole concept of process flow versus management objectives is exemplified by Juran.

Juran is strongly against 'campaigns to motivate the workforce to solve the company's quality problems by doing perfect work.' In his view slogans and motivation alone 'fail to set specific goals, establish specific plans to meet these goals, or provide the needed resources'. These approaches merely suit the executive desire to delegate quality to others.

The concepts taught by Juran are in the lexicon of all those today involved in TQM. They are now easy to accept, and to some extent familiarity breeds contempt. At the time Juran first promulgated his ideas they were contrary to managerial practice and were anathema to traditional quality managers. The authors believe that management's debt to Juran is immense; he was undoubtedly the first to bring a series of disconnected approaches into the cohesive whole that we now label TQM, though he then called it quality control.

Control has many meanings, but Juran defines it most simply as 'the totality of all the means by which we establish and achieve standards'. Whenever we decide to do something, we begin with a plan, work according to the plan, and review the results. If the results are not as planned we revise the work procedures or the plan, depending upon which is at fault. Juran relates quality control on company-wide quality management to the systemic methods used to meet business or financial goals. He talks of a 'trilogy' of basic managerial processes through which to manage quality. He compares his quality trilogy with financial terminology thus:

Trilogy Processes	Financial Terminology
Quality Planning	Budgeting, business planning
Quality control	Cost control, expense control, inventory control
Quality improvement	Cost reduction, profit improvement

He makes the point that, over the centuries, companies that have used the above financial approach have outperformed those that did not. The companies that use the same approach to quality will outperform those that do not.

Juran outlines the systemic approach to company-wide quality management as follows:

- Establish policies and goals for quality.
- Establish plans for meeting these quality goals.
- Provide the resources to evaluate progress against the goals and take appropriate action.
- Provide motivation to stimulate people to meet the goal.

Juran further states, 'The fact that a goal is set does not prove that it will be met; to meet it may require a significant improvement over past performance. The process for establishing goals includes a degree of voluntarism and negotiation. Quality goals are neither uniform nor static. They vary from one organisation to another, and from one year to the next.'

In some areas Juran differs significantly from the other gurus. He is not in favour of single sourcing for key purchases: 'For important purchases it is well to use multiple sources of supply. A single source can more easily neglect to sharpen its competitive edge in quality, cost and service.' He is, however, in favour of a close relationship with suppliers and believes they should be part of the team involved in quality improvement.

The Dow Chemicals comparison of the gurus, *Quality Coaches* highlights some further differences in the Juran approach. He is in favour of the concept of quality circles because they improve communications between management and labour. He also recommends using statistical process control, though he warns that it can lead to a 'tool oriented' approach. Juran does not believe that 'quality is free.' He explains that because of the law of diminishing returns, there is an optimum point of quality, beyond which conformance is more costly than the value of the quality obtained.

Juran is also more optimistic than Deming that the USA can catch up with the Japanese relatively soon. He feels that even the largest companies could complete top-down training in five years, not the fifteen years that it took in Japan. 'The Japanese fumbled around a lot,' he notes. 'I think our people are better poised to do it on a planned basis.' Deming thinks that it will take thirty years.

The Juran Institute in Wilton, Connecticut produces video cassettes and develops teaching materials for clients. A number of consultants worldwide are 'licensed' to teach his methods and use the centrally produced materials. They teach a project-by-project approach to quality improvement. Juran says, 'The project approach is important. When it comes to quality, there is no such thing as improvement in general. Any improvement in quality is going to come about project-by-project and no other way.'

It is interesting to note that according to David Hutchins, the Juran consultant in the UK, the level of Juran materials and video cassettes marketed in Britain is higher than for any other country. Perhaps the British are a more project-oriented nation.

Juran, like the other gurus, has his shorthand for quality improvement, which he encapsulates as follows:

Juran's Ten Steps to Quality Improvement

1 Build awareness of the need and opportunity for improvement.
2 Set goals for improvement.
3 Organise to reach the goals (establish a quality council, identify problems, select projects, appoint teams, designate facilitators).
4 Provide training.
5 Carry out projects to solve problems.
6 Report progress.
7 Give recognition.
8 Communicate results.
9 Keep score.
10 Maintain momentum by making annual improvement part of the regular systems and processes of the company.

19   The implementers

There are a number of other individuals, both American and Japanese, who have contributed to thought on quality without quite reaching the eminence of the three main gurus. Without any disrespect they can be described as minor gurus. Many were first inspired by one of the main gurus (Deming's influence on William E. Conway is a good example) but had the independence of mind to develop ideas of their own which disagreed with or emphasised a different direction than from their mentors'. In nearly every case these independent views were forged on the hard anvil of experience. In that sense the minor gurus can be categorised as the implementers.

To date no guru, major or minor, has emerged in Britain. In the authors' judgement that accolade can only be given to those who have contributed original thought to the concepts of TQM or demonstrated new paths to implementation. There certainly are many 'young pretenders' in the sense that a number of British practitioners have written books on aspects of quality management. However, these writers are generally commentators on the gurus or translators of their ideas to fit a British culture. This is not to disparage their contributions, but only to state that the word guru should not be loosely thrown about. Perhaps, for once, we British are too late onto the field of battle!

Several hundred books have been written about quality in all its aspects. One of the present authors, at the last count, had over seventy titles in his library, and thus had only scratched the surface. Some of these books had major impact, others caused a pause for thought and many are best forgotten. To select a few individuals who have influenced thought or added to knowledge in this field is inevitably a subjective exercise; hence we make no apologies for presenting our selection in alphabetical order:

William E. Conway
Armand V. Feigenbaum

H. James Harrington
Masaaki Imai
Kaoru Ishikawa
Shigeru Mizuno
Richard J. Schonberger
Genichi Taguchi

The last-named deserves a small chapter of his own, but as to the others, once again the bookshelf is perused and one can only reflect with Milton on blindness and say, 'They also serve who only stand and wait.'

Conway

As President and Chairman of the Nashua Corporation in 1979, William E. Conway invited Dr Deming to help improve the corporation's quality. Conway worked with Deming at Nashua for three years and steadily began to develop his own ideas on the management of quality improvement. In 1983 he formed Conway Quality Inc and has since then been an important influence.

Conway did not need an 'elevator speech' to convince him of the importance of quality. He was at the top himself and therefore had a different perspective. He talks of the 'right way to manage' and a 'new system of management' rather than quality improvement. His experience and broader perspective from the point of view of management permeates all his work. He agrees with the gurus that the biggest problem is that top management is not convinced that quality increases productivity and lowers cost. However, he also recognises that 'management wants and needs real help – not destructive criticism'.

Conway focuses on the management system as the means to achieve continuous improvement, rather than on specific functions or quality problems. Reading Conway led the author to his own view that TQM is not the objective but rather the *agent* of change which will help an organisation achieve the business objective of total continuous improvement.

Conway is a proponent of statistical methods. He says that management views quality in generalities. 'The use of statistics is a commonsense way of getting into specifics,' he says, and adds, 'Statistics don't solve problems' They identify where the problems are and point managers and people towards solutions'. He sees statistical techniques as management tools and urges the use of the simple statistical tools which everyone can quickly learn, rather than the sophisticated techniques. The simple tools can help solve 85 per cent of the problems. He also recommends the following basic tools for quality improvement:

1   Human relations skills – the responsibility of management to create at every level, among all employees, the motivation and training to make the necessary improvements in the organisation.

2   Statistical surveys – the gathering of data about customers (internal as well as external), employees, technology and equipment, to be used as a measure for future progress and to identify what needs to be done.

3   Simple statistical techniques – clear charts and diagrams that help identify problems, track work flow, gauge progress, and indicate solutions.

4   Statistical process control – the statistical charting of a process, whether manufacturing or non-manufacturing, to help identify and reduce variation.

5   Imagineering – a key concept in problem solving, involving the visualisation of a process, procedure or operation with all waste eliminated.

6   Industrial engineering – common techniques of pacing, work simplification, methods analysis, plant layout and material handling to achieve improvements.

Feigenbaum

Armand V. Feigenbaum marked an important step in the evolution of quality management when he first used the word 'total' in conjunction with quality. He was manager of manufacturing operations and worldwide quality for the General Electric Company of the USA when he published the first edition of his book *Total Quality Control* in 1961. In the late sixties he established the General Systems Company Inc in Pittsfield, Massachusetts, which designs and implements integrated operational systems for improving quality.

He is little known to general managers but is considered essential reading for quality specialists. A continually updated tome of close to a thousand pages *Total Quality Control* is considered a 'bible' by many quality managers. Jeremy Main, in his *Fortune* magazine article on the gurus, describes him thus: 'A serious, unexciting engineer, Feigenbaum . . . delivers no uplifting messages to eager executives. He is more likely to put them asleep with a style that even his admirers find soporific.'

Feigenbaum says that the quality of products and services is directly influenced in nine basic areas, or what he calls the 'Nine Ms'. They are:

1   *Markets:* The number of new and improved products offered in the marketplace continues to grow at an explosive rate. Consumer wants

and needs are carefully identified by today's businesses as a basis for developing new products. For an increasing number of companies, markets are international and even worldwide. As a result, businesses must be highly flexible and able to change direction rapidly.

2 *Money:* The increase of competition in many fields, coupled with worldwide economic fluctuations, has shaved profit margins. At the same time, the need for automation and mechanisation has forced large outlays for new equipment and processes. Quality costs associated with the maintenance and improvement of quality have reached unprecedented heights. This fact has focused the attention of managers on the quality-cost areas as one of the 'soft spots' in which operating costs and losses can be decreased to improve profits.

3 *Management:* Responsibility for quality has been distributed among several specialised groups. Quality Control must plan the quality measurements throughout the process flow which will ensure that the end result will meet quality requirements. And quality of service, after the product has reached the customer, has become an increasingly important part of the total 'product package'. This has increased the load upon top management, particularly in view of the increased difficulty of allocating proper responsibility for correcting departure from quality standards.

4 *Men:* The rapid growth in technical knowledge and the origination of whole new fields such as computer electronics have created a great demand for workers with specialised knowledge. Although specialisation has its advantages, its disadvantage is breaking the responsibility for product quality into a number of pieces. The numerous aspects of business operating systems have become the focus of modern management.

5 *Motivation:* The increased complexity of getting a quality product to market has magnified the importance of the quality contribution of every employee. Human motivational research has shown that in addition to monetary reward, today's workers require reinforcement of a sense of accomplishment in their jobs and the positive recognition that they are personally contributing to achievement of company goals. This has led to an unprecedented need for quality education and for improved communication of quality-consciousness.

6 *Materials:* Owing to production costs and quality requirements, engineers are working materials to closer limits than ever before and using many new, so-called exotic metals and alloys for special applications. The visual inspection and thickness check of a few years ago is no longer acceptable.

7   *Machines and mechanisation:* The demand of companies to get cost reductions and production volume to satisfy the customer in intensely competitive markets has forced the use of manufacturing equipment which is steadily becoming more complex and much more dependent upon the quality of material fed into it. Good quality is becoming a critical factor in maintaining machine 'up' time for full utilisation of facilities.

8   *Modern information methods:* The rapid evolution of computer technology has made possible the collection, storage, retrieval, and manipulation of information on a scale never before imaginable.

9   *Mounting product requirements:* Great advances in the intricacy of engineering designs, demanding much closer control over manufacturing processes, have made the formerly ignored 'little things' of great potential importance.

Harrington

Dr H. James Harrington is a recent entry to the list of implementers or minor gurus. A quality executive with IBM, Harrington has produced several papers of interest describing the progress of the quality revolution at IBM. In 1987 he brought together that experience and the efforts of other organisations in his book *The Improvement Process*.

He makes it clear that the only approach to quality that will succeed is one that makes it *the* predominant way of life in the corporation. Like Conway, he emphasises that quaility grows out of a management style and not just a series of techniques or worker motivation. Management is to use these techniques as tools. Harrington emphasises the importance of management 'ownership' of processes, crossing departmental barriers. As well as highlighting the role of senior management, he develops a new role for the first-line supervisor. He considers the supervisor the key to successful implementation of the improvement process.

His book is a highly detailed, but easily read, step-by-step guide to the implementation of quality improvement in a modern Western company.

Imai

Masaaki Imai is Chairman of the Cambridge Corporation, an internatinal management consulting firm based in Tokyo which he founded in 1962. He advises both Western and Japanese companies.

He is the author of several books, but the most influential is *Kaizen*, published in 1986. He sees *Kaizen* as 'a single and readily understandable concept which brings together the management philosophies, theories and tools that have been developed over the years in Japan.' He calls this 'the *Kaizen* umbrella'.

He has worked closely with Ishikawa and the former Toyota vice president Taiichi Ohno, who initiated the 'just in time' system. He also spent five years at the Japan Productivity Centre in Washington, DC, studying American management practices and helping to introduce them into Japan. The Japanese have developed these practices further, and now Imai is bringing the improved versions back to the West.

Ishikawa

Professor Kaoru Ishikawa, late president of the Musashi Institute of Technology, really ranks as a major guru and is certainly the best known of the Japanese contributors to the theory of quality management.

He is best known to Western management as the originator of the Ishikawa cause and effect diagram, sometimes called the fishbone diagram because of its resemblance to a fish skeleton. This approach to problem solving is the most widely taught and used technique for analysing the likely causes of a known effect.

The quotation in Chapter 1 defining the Japanese approach to quality management indicates that Ishikawa's influence and contribution goes way beyond the invention of a specific technique. He defined the management philosophy behind quality, the elements of quality systems and what he calls the 'seven basic tools' of quality management, which are:

1 Process flow charting   what is done
2 Tally charts   how often it is done
3 Histograms   pictorial view of variation
4 Pareto analysis   rating of problems
5 Cause and effect analysis   what causes problems
6 Scatter diagrams   defining relationships
7 Control charts   measuring and controlling variation

Mizuno

Professor Shigeru Mizuno is little known outside his own country, but his writing is now reaching the West. However, he is widely recognised in Japan and has received many awards and honours for his contribution to industrial productivity and the nation's economic success. He is fundamentally an academic but has also served as a director of the Union of Japanese Scientists and Engineers (the group that first invited Deming to Japan), advisor to the Central Japan Quality Control Association, and chairman of the Quality Management Laboratory.

Mizuno is not really an initiator like his colleague Ishikawa or the American gurus, but a clear and systematic definer of the practical steps to the implementation of quality management. His book *Company Wide Total Quality Control*, first published in Japan in 1984, is a concise guide to implementation. Unlike many books of its kind, it is easily understood by the manager new to the subject and is packed with practical examples.

Schonberger

Richard J. Schonberger is a world-renowned authority on production and manufacturing. He is president of his own consulting firm, Schonberger and Associates, based in Seattle, Washington in the USA. His is a wider spectrum than quality, but the management of quality strategies is a central element of his writing.

His best-selling book *Japanese Manufacturing Techniques* had a major impact on American manufacturing theory. He was one of the first to demystify and explain what the Japanese were really doing. He demonstrated that their success had little to do with national culture and that the relatively simple Japanese techniques could be used just as easily in America.

Schonberger's more recent book *World Class Manufacturing* looks at how 'the lessons of simplicity' have been applied in a substantial number of American corporations. He also shows that these lessons from Japan apply equally to all industries and businesses. He describes these companies as the '5-10-20s' where manufacturing lead times have been reduced fivefold, tenfold and twentyfold. The ability to respond to changing market needs is a constant theme for modern business, Schonberger maintains.

Schonberger provides what he calls an 'action agenda for manufacturing excellence' of seventeen items:

1 Get to know the customer.
2 Cut work in process.
3 Cut flow times.
4 Cut setup and changeover times.
5 Cut flow distance and space.

6   Increase make/deliver frequency for each required item.

7   Cut number of suppliers down to a few good ones.

8   Cut number of part numbers.

9   Make it easy to manufacture the product without error.

10   Arrange the workplace to eliminate search time.

11   Cross-train for mastery of more than one job.

12   Record and retain production, quality and problem data at the workplace.

13   Assure that line people get first crack at problem solving – before experts.

14   Maintain and improve existing equipment and human work before thinking about new equipment.

15   Look for simple, cheap and movable equipment.

16   Seek to have plural instead of singular work stations, machines, cells and lines for each product.

17   Automate incrementally, when process variability cannot otherwise be reduced.

In reality these agenda items represent a series of practical steps in the application of quality-first thinking to the manufacturing workplace.

All the implementers or commentators highlighted in this chapter have concentrated on simple techniques and methodologies. One other guru, Genichi Taguchi, is at the other end of the scale of sophistication. He is the main subject of the next chapter.

20 *I didn't understand a word he said, but . . .!*

Quality management can become very sophisticated, and a leading exponent of sophistication is Genichi Taguchi, a Japanese engineering specialist who acts as a consultant to leading Japanese and American high-technology companies. Taguchi is not easy to understand even for reasonably sophisticated engineers, let alone general managers.

Jeremy Main, in his previously quoted *Fortune* article on the gurus, reports that when Bell Laboratories invited Taguchi to describe his statistical methods to them they didn't understand a word he said. They assumed at first that the problem was his command of English. But when they asked some Japanese scientists about Taguchi, it turned out that his own countrymen had difficulty understanding him. Later, Bell asked him to work with them on the design of a manufacturing process for a new integrated circuit. Within six weeks Taguchi had helped Bell cut the defect rate on the circuits by half. Bell still didn't understand exactly what he had done, but it liked the results and has been inviting him back ever since.

Taguchi's statistical methods are particularly difficult to assimilate. For example, his two-volume work on his 'System of Experimental Design' amounts to 1177 pages, and there is probably not one page without some algebraic formula or mathematical expression. This is not easy bedtime reading. However, behind his statistical method lie some important philosophies on quality.

In the present marketing and political environment he may be seen as the first 'green guru'. He teaches that an important factor in the quality of a product or service is the total loss to society that it can generate. He argues that few products that are designed to perform the same function or meet the same customer need can do so without also causing similar losses to society when in use. In other words, there is not only manufacturing cost, after-sales service cost and other default costs to the individual customer to be considered; there are also costs to society as a whole.

Taguchi, however is not concerned only with 'green' issues in saying that quality control is concerned with reducing the social or environmental loss that the product may cause through its instrinsic function. For example, he points out that liquor has the function of intoxication, and that substantial losses are caused to society by inebriation, but argues that it is a nonsense to manufacture non-intoxicating liquor because the resulting product simply would not be liquor. (The authors feel the same about so-called alcohol-free lager!) Taguchi's method of analysing quality, known as 'total loss function', addresses one of the issues discussed in Chapter 8: the way in which the customer's perception is now extending to awareness of the *full* cost of a product.

Taguchi sees quality as inversely related to 'the loss imported to society from the time a product is shipped'. This concept is really designed to mesh with the statistical method he uses to calculate total loss (this book is not the place to discuss how he works out deviation from the 'optimum target value') and it ignores losses to society incurred during manufacture of the product. It is also somewhat too difficult to calculate for its use to become widespread. However, it does force a new way of thinking about intrinsic product quality. As Taguchi himself says, 'If quality is designed as the loss a product causes to society, then automobile exhaust, air conditioner noise, toxic gas from incinerating plastic containers and all other pollution problems that cause third-party losses are quality problems. Since the third party is not the purchaser of the product, he does not receive any of the utility, all he gets is the loss.'

Taguchi's other major contribution to thinking about quality is to focus attention on the original design phases of a product or service. He argues that the prevention of problems, both in the manufacture of a product and in its use, must be built in at the design stage. The concept is not new but it has always been very expensive in practice. Prototypes, for example, are design experiments preceding full production, but by their nature ignore many factors in the real-life manufacture and use of a product. Taguchi has developed statistical methods for what he calls 'off line' quality control. Off-line quality management concentrates on the design process, while on-line quality control concentrates on the manufacture of the product. His statistical approach to the off-line management of quality is now generally referred to as 'design of experiments'.

Apart from the statistical methods used by Taguchi, there are a number of other relatively sophisticated tools or techniques used in quality management. The most commonly mentioned are:

FMEA   Failure Mode and Effect Analysis, used to study potential
       failures to determine their likely effects so that prevention
       can be planned.

QFD   Quality Functional Deployment, a collective title for a
       number of systems and documentation methods devised to
       assist the design process and help meet customer
       requirements.

These and many other tools mentioned in this book will increase the
future utilisation of the professional quality manager. There has been a
tendency in recent years to decry his function in the company. The need
to involve management at the highest level in quality and to generally
change management behaviour and the attitudes of all employees has
taken quality, in the minds of many, away from the quality
professionals. The authors agree with the new approach but still value
the contribution of the quality professional.

In the past, the quality professional was seen as *the* individual
responsible for quality. It was considered *his* fault if quality was not
achieved. But that was never true, though some quality managers
undermined their own cause by acting as if they believed it was true. The
quality professionals are in the same position as every other function;
they are working in the process and can therefore only affect some 20 per
cent of the problems. In reality, they are specialists in measurement
techniques and systems which can assist management in the
improvement of quality.

Deming may want every manager to become numerate and
statistically literate, but in the short-term he is whistling in the dark. As
the techniques and tools become more sophisticated, the manager will
come to rely on the quality professional. Managers must certainly
become more numerate in the sense that they understand the value and
objectives of the techniques, if only so that they can communicate with
the specialists. They will not need to be able to operate all the techniques.
The majority of modern managers now understand the benefits and
outcomes of fairly sophisticated computers. The same will be true of
sophisticated quality management techniques. Managers will say, as the
irate politician might have said, 'Don't give me the facts, give me the
truth!' The problem in the past was that all the quality manager could do
was to give management a host of facts, never the truth – that poor
quality was management's fault.

21 A collective wisdom

Executives who have accepted the need to change their approach to quality now want to implement TQM in their own organisations. They are determined to get it right in their own companies and have therefore studied the various gurus or discussed their approaches with consultants. They may also have looked at the experience of other companies. They will almost certainly have received conflicting advice. They are now faced with a difficult decision which will probably be based on their answers to the following questions:

- Do the concepts, teaching and implementation approach of one particular guru uniquely fit our circumstances?
- Is it possible to find a 'golden thread' or to select the best from each guru to create some form of collective wisdom?
- Whichever course we adopt, should we try to 'do our own thing' or should we seek outside help?
- If we decide to accept outside help, which consultant is best suited to our culture?

In Chapter 5 the authors touched upon some of the issues involved in answering the last question. We have no intention of providing a definitive answer; there are too many subjective issues surrounding the question. We do believe, however, that most companies will need outside help, and our reasons for that viewpoint will be developed in Chapter 25.

We have reached our own conclusions in answer to the first two key questions, regarding the selection of gurus or a collective wisdom, and the whole of Part Three of this book outlines our approach to the actions needed to implement TQM. However, we do not claim to be gurus and do not have the arrogance to believe that our answers will automatically meet the needs of every organisation. We can only claim to be enthusiastic travellers on the road to total continuous improvement. As such, we have met obstacles which we have overcome, and other obstacles where we have fallen, brushed ourselves down and then started again. For these reasons the arguments advanced in the rest of this chapter would be better viewed as resulting from shared experience rather than profound wisdom, collective or otherwise.

Total quality management is not a fixed method of management (if there is such a thing) which can be taught to all. It is not even a fixed objective for management. TQM is evolving and it is evolving rapidly. The fixed objective for management may be seen as a total continuous improvement, and TQM itself as the agent of change to assist management to get from where they are to where they want to be.

Every company is starting from a different position in relation to the final objective. In every company the level of customer orientation, the communication culture, the behaviour of management and the attitudes of employees to quality will differ. The business culture is also evolving. In that situation it is not reasonable to expect one methodology to fit all circumstances.

There is a unifying thread in the broad philosophies of all the gurus and most of the consultants. It is in their approach to implementation or methodology that the difficulties occur. Fourteen of this, nine of that or seven of something else can sometimes resemble a number of pharmaceutical companies offering different cures for the common cold. They may all do you some good, but it is difficult to tell which one, if any, offers the complete cure. In the case of TQM everyone selects their own favourite remedy, but perhaps in reality it is their own recuperative energies which effect the cure.

The collective wisdom of the gurus is enshrined in the concepts which are common to all of them. These can be summarised as follows:

- The process of change must start with top management.
- The change is cultural in the sense that it demands a different kind of behaviour from management and a resulting change in employee attitude.
- Quality and business operations are indivisible; quality is not a separate, delegated function.
- Quality is achieved through people more than through technology, specific systems or tools.
- Quality involves everyone in the organisation.
- The change cannot be achieved by motivation alone, though the motivation of people is an essential element.

- Education and training for everyone in the organisation is a prerequisite for achieving a lasting environment for improvement.
- Continuous improvement requires commitment and constancy of purpose from senior management.

The areas of disagreement or differing areas of emphasis occur in the methods and actions proposed to achieve all the above.

In an evolutionary business and TQM environment the new and intrepid voyager should beware of sirens who seem to have every answer but could land the process on the rocks. In the opinion of the authors the issues for careful consideration are as follows:

- The methodology must be flexible enough to fit the organisation.
- A general approach or a project-by-project approach are equally viable, depending on the culture of the company.
- A project-by-project approach must also involve an overall change in management behaviour and employee attitudes. The chosen approach must ensure that quality becomes part of 'the woodwork'.
- Educational courses and materials for internal use must be capable of adaptation to fit the environment. Remember that the aim in your company is to take into account the changing needs of the customers and to delight them, and in this situation you are the customer. Insist that the consultants, who are your suppliers, practice what they preach and meet your needs.
- Statistical methodology, total implementation systems or other sophisticated tools are valuable, but they are only part of the solution. Do not be bemused by tools and systems.

A final conclusion worth bearing in mind: history has taught us that gurus are not always the easiest people to work with. Their confidence in their own opinions can sometimes be overpowering. They have a tendency to believe that the elephant sits down where it wants to sit down. Dodging an elephant from chair to chair can inhibit creative thought.

PART THREE

The Actions

The practical actions needed to implement
total quality management.

22 Getting started

How to get started on the long road to continuous improvement is the first obstacle facing the management of a company. The decision to start may come from the chief executive, or may be recommended by divisional or middle management. It is more often based on a vision of the future, or the company's destination. Those involved may have only the vaguest idea of the perils to be faced on the journey.

The vision must be maintained, even heightened, to ensure that a constancy of purpose exists. Everyone in the organisation must be pulled by their customer orientation rather than pushed by executive decree. But knowledge of the route will ease the journey, bridge the gaps and provide clear signposts for everyone in the company. Teamwork starts at the top. The first step on the journey is to ensure that all the executives and senior management are aware of the destination and the nature of the road.

The chief executive should start the journey by organising an awareness session to introduce his colleagues to the guiding concepts. It is vital that this be led by someone who wholly understands the concepts, and has knowledge and experience of implementing the process of total quality management. He could come from an outside consultant company or be a quality leader from a company that has successfully implemented the process.

Introducing change into an organisation is a difficult and challenging process. Resistance to change is natural. There are many ostensibly good reasons that can be evidenced to discourage innovation. Resistors will tend to use phrases such as, 'I hear what you are saying, but . . .' The best way to overcome this resistance is to ensure that the senior management *take ownership of the need to change* within their own operation or company – that is, take the goal of change to heart and make it completely their own rather than something imposed from outside.

The objective of the awareness session is divided into three parts:

1 To achieve some recognition of the need to change, even though more work will be needed for all to take complete ownership.

2   To ensure that the executives have a reasonable comprehension of the concepts that lie behind total quality management.

3   To give the executives a clear sense of what is involved in the quality improvement process, and in particular what is required of them.

The awareness session will involve all the senior management in the desire, indeed the need, to begin the journey. They will now realise that the implementation of total quality management is a massive task. This realisation will grow into the understanding that this is the biggest project yet undertaken by the company. It is, almost certainly, the first project to involve every employee. The process is going to change the culture, the very fibre of the company. It is of sufficient priority to require the close attention of senior management. The task will also need careful planning and preparation.

To focus the attention of senior management from the outset, a Quality Steering Committee (QSC) should be formed. The QSC is in reality the Board or the principal operating committee meeting separately to focus entirely on quality. The committee should be chaired by the managing director or the chief executive. The members should be his key direct reports, representing all the major functions or divisions of the company. If the process is started as a pilot programme in a division or strategic business unit of a major corporation, a similarly structured Quality Steering Committee should be established, with the divisional head as chairman. The purpose of the QSC is to ensure that the requisite planning is carried out, that resources are provided and that the whole process is led from the top.

The first meeting of the QSC should organise a full assessment of the company's position in relation to quality. This is an essential preparation for the detailed planning stage which will create a strategy for quality improvement. The assessment will also reinforce awareness of the need, and thus will lead to a stronger commitment on the part of the senior management. They will have a deeper comprehension of where the company really stands in relation to its competition, its customers and its employees.

The same meeting should also consider the appointment of a TQM co-ordinator or 'Quality Champion'. This is an extremely important decision and needs to be considered carefully. Ideally the TQM co-ordinator should be appointed before the assessment phase; it will help prepare him for this assignment and will assist the committee. In any case he must be appointed before the detailed planning stage.

The company has now given the implementation of TQM the first priority. The TQM co-ordinator will be responsible to the Quality Steering Committee for co-ordinating the process of change. He will also be representing the disparate parts of the process to the Committee. To ensure that he has the necessary authority and influence, he should report directly to the chairman of the committee.

This is a senior management appointment. The post demands considerable organisational skills and high communicative abilities. An important factor in the selection of the candidate is the initial impact the appointment will have on the organisation. The message to the company as a whole must show how serious the chief executive's commitment to quality is. The worst decision is to treat it as a 'library job', or a safe haven for a senior individual coasting to retirement. The best decision is to appoint a recognised candidate for seniority. The extensive spread of responsibility and span of influence makes the job an ideal proving ground for general management. The message to aspiring senior managers would also be loud and clear.

Some gurus advise against appointing the current head of quality to the post. This relates directly to the message; it could be seen as an indication that nothing has changed, irrespective of the abilities of the individual in question. However, if the head of quality already reports to the chief executive and he has the ability, his appointment should be seriously considered and represented as a promotion. It should not be forgotten that the technical skills of the quality operations are vital to the process. It is also worth noting that two of the most influential gurus, Philip B. Crosby and Armand V. Feigenbaum, essentially and very effectively trod this path, for ITT and General Electric respectively. Maybe they were the exceptions that prove the rule!

Management Commitment

Management commitment has been mentioned before and will be mentioned again. The importance of management commitment cannot be over-emphasised. The whole success of the enterprise stands or falls on the level of management commitment and leadership given to the TQM process. Management will need to be brave and above all consistent.

Management must lead the process by:

- Defining the constant purpose of the organisation and the improvement principles and values.
- Ensuring that there is a continuous programme of education and self-improvement for everyone.
- Removing all the barriers that prevent quality being achieved through people.
- Providing the necessary resources.
- Ensuring that their actions demonstrate the integrity of the continuous improvement process.

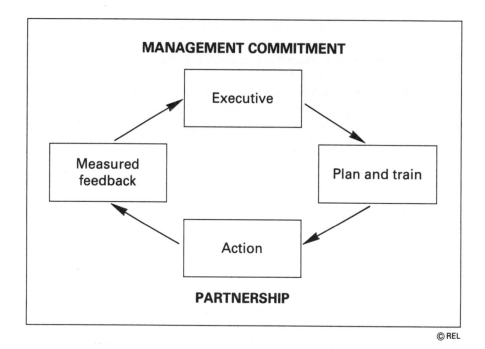

© REL

Figure 23   *Management commitment creates a partnership with all in the company.*

The role of management in the leadership process is clear but there is more to management commitment than the above would indicate. Management must be actively involved with the workforce in improving work processes. It is impossible for the workers to accomplish more than relatively minor improvements without the involvement and co-operation of management. Shewhart demonstrated through statistical concepts that people *work in* the process and that management *works on* the process. Only management has control of the resources to ensure that the people are fully trained and to provide the right equipment and facilities so that the process can meet the customer's requirements.

The people working in the process can certainly measure or indicate what is wrong with a work process. If given permission they can inform management. But management must provide the resources for correction or improvement. As resources are scarce and must be controlled, management must involve themselves in the process.

The implications of management's role in leading the TQM process and becoming actively involved in improvement activities will become clearer as we proceed. But first we must start with the company assessment.

23   Mirror, mirror on the wall

The management team, organised as the Quality Steering Committee or QSC, must start with an assessment of the company's current position in relation to quality. When planning a route to a given destination, it is essential to know first where you are.

Management has to realise that this is going to be a long journey, extending over years – in fact never ending. Many obstacles will be met on the way. Management will be inviting all their employees to follow the same route. Route instructions may be misunderstood by some, lost by others. The original route planners may well have gone, long before the destination is in sight. All of these factors can lead to diversion and weakening of the constancy of purpose. Management must be capable of monitoring progress and taking corrective action where necessary. The purpose, therefore, of the assessment is to establish from the outset a series of benchmarks or milestones to measure progress.

Failure to make this assessment is the most common fault found in organisations which are having problems with TQM. Lack of management commitment is most often cited as the main reason for failure, but in the authors' experience it is usually failure to establish criteria for measurement that has caused the fall-off in management commitment. Management just did not know that they had left the road. They must not arrive at the position of the man who, when asked the way to Rome, replied: 'I wouldn't start from here.'

The senior executives of an organisation will generally be involved in three levels of assessment. It would be advantageous to engage an experienced outsider to assist them at each level. These levels can be described as follows:

- A broad 'toe in the water' assessment of the company's position. This is usually part of the awareness session and is designed to assist in the discovery of the need to change.
- A more detailed assessment, which will look at more factors impacting the introduction of TQM. This should include an estimate

of the quality costs, customers' perception of the company, competitive position and employee attitudes. If relevant data do not exist in the company, much of this assessment will still rely on executive opinion. However, the executives can now develop a broad strategy for the quality improvement process.

● A third stage, which requires organised data needed to establish the measurement criteria for the final business plan outlining the implementation of TQM. The executives are likely to assign the task of developing this data to the TQM co-ordinator.

The education of management (facilitators) who will be involved in the managing of the process will begin after the second-level assessment. They will thus be in a position to assist with the detailed assessments. Let's look at each of these levels in more depth.

First-Level Assessment

The first-level assessment really starts the thinking process as to where the organisation stands against some external criteria. This usually takes the form of a grid (see Figure 24) on which individual executives rate their company in a series of categories. The individual results are summarised (anonymously) and shown to the group. A group of executives from the same company will often receive their first shock at this stage. There can be a wide divergence of opinion amongst people who have been working closely together towards a common goal. For the conceptualists, this brings an immediate recognition that quality is a 'people issue'. It also poses the question: 'If we differ to this degree as to where our company stands, how does the rest of the organisation perceive the position?' – a powerful and salutary preparation for the start of the process of change.

The same grid used by the executives can also be utilised as a simple measurement device. If the grid forms part of the educational material used to introduce TQM to everyone in the organisation, the summarised results can be reviewed from time to time on the QSC. As education cascades down through the ranks the grid results will be a useful pointer to the success of the initial awareness campaign.

Second-Level Assessment

The objective of the second-level assessment is to help the Quality Steering Committee prepare to develop the broad strategy for the organisation's TQM process. The assessment will establish the level of waste

Please show your answers to each question by ticking one of the boxes.				
POOR	**MODERATE**	**AVERAGE**	**GOOD**	**EXCELLENT**
1 How I rate our services versus the competition's				
We are struggling – sell by price alone ☐	Not too bad – we have some good features ☐	Reasonable standard – no serious problems ☐	Up to industry standards ☐	Best in the industry – always delight the customer ☐
2 How I believe our customers perceive us				
Customer complaints are a serious problem ☐	We usually sort out customer problems ☐	Not too many complaints ☐	They keep coming back – must like us ☐	We keep in close contact – delighted with us ☐
3 How I belive our suppliers see us				
Never know what they want – bad payers ☐	Do not always know what they want – otherwise OK ☐	No problem but always price dominated ☐	Usually know what they want – easy to work with ☐	Absolutely clear requirements – a real partnership ☐
4 How I believe employees see the company				
Never know where you are – can't make up their minds ☐	Not too bad as employers go ☐	Always fair – no complaints ☐	A good company ☐	Proud to be with us ☐
5 How I believe the competition views us				
Forgotten they were still in the market ☐	Pick up some of their dissatisfied customers ☐	Pretty good – we win some, we lose some ☐	Tough competitors ☐	Out of our league ☐

© REL

Figure 24 *A typical management perception assessment form.*

in the organisation and probe more deeply into senior management's opinions and views as to the best approach for their organisation. The process will increase comprehension of the need to change, and thus strengthen the commitment to do so. It will also clarify those areas where more factual data is required for the establishment of a detailed business plan for the implementation of TQM.

Hopefully, the TQM co-ordinator will have been appointed by now and will be a member of the QSC. Depending on the size of the company, some additional plant or locational general managers may be involved at this stage. The TQM co-ordinator could act as a moderator but, at this stage, there is some danger of the blind leading the blind. Generally, it is wiser to use an experienced TQM consultant.

The time expended on this exericse should not be excessive, and it would usually be completed within five to ten days. Two meetings of the QSC should be interspersed with a series of individual meetings between the consultant and operational managers. Some operational managers may wish to involve their direct reports in the process. The financial director and his staff will have more involvement in helping to establish the quality costs.

The consultant will lead the initial meeting of the QSC through a quick reprise of the main principles of TQM and then develop the concept of the cost of quality in greater detail. He will provide each member of the Committee with a guide to those processes in each function of the organisation where waste is most likely to appear. He will ask them to individually consider the relevant process in their respective domains and arrange a schedule of interviews. He will emphasise that the operational managers should concern themselves with the time expended on chasing problems, redoing tasks and communications hassles. They will not be asked to calculate all the costs and overheads involved.

The consultant will then spend some time with the financial director or his staff to explain how the costs will be calculated and provide some simple forms for this process. A member of the financial department will accompany the consultant at each interview, recording the areas identified for later calculation. During his time with the financial department, the consultant will be able to identify some immediate figures that can be directly attributed to failure costs. The company cost codes will contain whole accounts which can be posted to failure. These will include such accounts as warranty, customer complaints department, rework, waste and premium freight. The financial director will have been included in the schedule of interviews. This may be completed now or at a later stage.

The individual meetings will usually be conducted in the manager's office. The consultant will act as a catalyst and listener. His questions should provoke discussion and highlight the areas of non-comformance.

Open discussion becomes easy once the manager is aware of the principle that where the costs are found is not necessarily where they are caused. All the areas identified will be recorded by the financial assistant. The consultant will also invite the manager to complete some simple questionnaires (probably distributed at the group meeting). These questionnaires will indicate attitudes to or perceptions of quality and customer–supplier relationships as well as the manager's view of his staff's attitudes. The consultant will also note any trenchant views that arise from the discussions, though he will use these later with discretion and anonymity.

At the completion of all the interviews, the financial team will calculate and collate all the quality costs identified. The financial director will prepare a presentation for the QSC. It is advisable for the organisation's finance department rather than the consultant to prepare and present these conclusions. The company looks to the financial director to present its financial position of the company; hence the QSC are more likely to accept responsibility for the costs when they are presented by their own financial leader.

The consultant will prepare a presentation of his assessment findings based on the questionnaires and comments made during the interviews. The presentation will be given at the reconvened QSC meeting, but first the financial director will present the cost-of-quality figures. Experience shows that this first-pass assessment of the cost of failure, appraisal and prevention will only identify some 50 per cent of the real figure. However, the amount uncovered is usually dramatic enough to provoke action. In any case, the fact that the committee have uncovered only a portion of the real wastage should be fairly obvious. Although most of these senior managers will have read of, or heard consultants quote, high figures for the cost of poor quality, they will not have really believed until now that figures like that could apply to *their* organisation.

The consultant's presentation of his assessment will, by its nature, highlight some of the underlying causes of this prodigal waste. Questionnaires will relate to customer and supplier perceptions and the company's competitive position in relation to quality. This procedure will usually lead to discussion and increasing consensus on areas of weakness.

Third-Level Assessment

As a result of this discussion the TQM co-ordinator may be instructed to organise detailed surveys into employee attitudes and customer and supplier perceptions as well as market research into the company's position. In the best of companies this data will already exist, but it may not have been considered in relation to quality.

The QSC is now ready to plan a strategy for the implementation of TQM. It should be done now; strike whilst the iron is hot and the need to change is uppermost in people's minds. Next week you may be up to your neck in alligators! However, there are some other fundamental issues to be developed before tackling the question of where the company is going.

24   *David and Goliath*

The principles of TQM remain the same, whatever the structure, size or nature of the organisation. However, the strategy for implementing the principles will be affected by these factors. An analysis of the type of company is an essential element in assessing the approach to be taken in implementing TQM.

A recurring theme of this book is cultural change, involving a change in management style and a change in employee attitude. The present culture has been largely determined by the nature of the organisation. Changing the culture requires that there is a thorough understanding of those factors within the company which influence the culture. Those influences lie buried within the organisation. They may arise and inhibit, or even support, the desired change. All these issues must be recognised, defined and accounted for in the business plan for TQM. Failure to do so may make implementation more difficult and fraught with needless pain.

Sheer size is not the only issue to be considered. The very nature of the business can have a crucial bearing on the structures of implementation. Consider an international car hire firm. It is a large firm, measured by either the total number of people employed or by sales revenue. The organisation will be distributed through hundreds, or even thousands, of locations, most very small but with an occasional large hub at an airport. Many of these locations will actually be agencies rather than staffed by direct employees, yet their quality of service will influence the customer's perception of the whole company. To an extent, process communication within the company is largely via computer terminals. In this case the management strategy for organising the process and creating a common attitude to quality obviously differs greatly from that of a similar-sized company organised on two or three locations.

Consider a large retail chain. Each location may employ sufficient people to provide a nucleus for locational quality improvement. The nature of these businesses also provides good communication with area and locational management. Most of the communication channels between locations and with distributors and suppliers *have* to be good to produce profit from the high volume–low margin business. So most factors are favourable for the implementation of TQM. But how do you educate the people so that all can contribute to the process? The nature of this business is massive turnover on Saturdays and perhaps one evening per week. The fluctuations in trade are bridged by temporary staff; on key days they may outnumber the permanent staff. The company cannot afford to educate temporary staff!

Well, can it afford not to? Not to do so would mean that the customer's primary contact will not delight him or her, on the one day that person deals with the business. Anyone who has shopped in London, or most other cities, at or around Christmas time will recognise the feeling. However, this is a very competitive business, which in the long run will depend on delighting its customers. Its executives know that, but they will have different concerns when planning their implementation strategy.

Another example to illustrate the point: Consider a large mainframe computer company. They will have a substantial customer services operation employing highly qualified electronic engineers. Their job is to install and maintain computer systems worth millions of pounds. Any downtime in these installations will have a deleterious effect on the customer's business. The quality of service given by these engineers is the key to how the customer views the company.

Some would argue that if the computers and their peripherals were quality products in the first place the company would not have this problem. That may be correct and the computer company's executives may believe it to be true. However, they are just starting the quality improvement process and in their wildest dreams, or however committed they are to the process, they are not going to change this situation overnight. So what's the implementation problem? By the nature of the business these engineers work in reactive mode; in other words they go into action when the computer breaks down. It is almost impossible to schedule meetings, let alone continuing educational sessions, for all of them. Yet involved they must be, if only for the reason that they know more about the problems with the product than anybody. Despite what many would think, they will be the most enthusiastic about the improvement process (once they see that it is not just the flavour of the month). The reason they will take this attitude is that they are having to work amid the hassle others are causing them; they also have been pointing this out to their management for years. But the nature of their work is another issue for the implementation plan.

A slight digression: the author joined the computer industry in the fifties. At that time the most repetitive product problems affecting computer performance came generally under the heading 'connectors'.

However, each instance was a relatively minor problem and could be 'fixed' by the maintenance engineer. These problems, though recognised as prevalent, were not considered sufficiently serious to penetrate through the blancmange of middle management to the design engineers. Some thirty years later, after the industry had spent billions of pounds on research and development, the most prevalent problems were still grouped under the heading 'connectors'. Little seems to change; the insignificant many always triumph over the significant few. The small problem which is easily fixed is rarely fixed for ever. With some ironic amusement, the author noted a similarity when he visited a vehicle assembly line in a major factory. The quality manager explained in answer to a question that his most prevalent problem was 'electrical connectors'! *C'est la vie!*

These examples have highlighted some problems that can be encountered when planning the strategy for change. They can all be surmounted if they have been considered at the planning stage.

These particular issues were linked to education and communication. The strategy will establish an organisation within the company whose primary responsibility will be to establish systems to facilitate communication and ensure that all receive the appropriate education. This TQM process organisation is purely facilitative. It is staffed by individuals who for the most part are still working in their current jobs. They don another hat for limited periods to help their colleagues engineer the change. They are never responsible for quality other than in their normal role. Every individual in the company will eventually be responsible for quality. The role of the TQM organisation (see Figure 25) is to manage the process of change in communication cultures – the

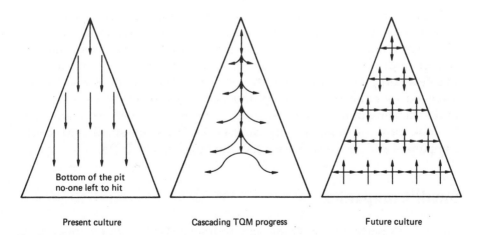

Figure 25 *The role of the TQM process in changing the communications culture.*

change from the present culture of predominantly vertical communication to a future culture of four-way communicating teams. This is the crux of the whole TQM process.

Typically, companies communicate down through departments or functions. To a large extent this communication is one way and is re-inforced by the way objectives and reward structures are established. Over time this culture has created fear in the organisation and erected barriers to real communication. The people at the bottom of the chain feel remote from the purpose of the organisation and believe that they have little influence on the success or failure of the business. They are passive onlookers, 'hammered' into submission and with no one below them to hit in turn. This feeling is exacerbated by the attitudes of middle managers, who as messengers exercise some influence and power. In many organisations middle management act as a blancmange of purposeful fog. They will distort the intended message or communicate only part of it downward and will exercise power by smothering the reply from below. At its worst this culture is responsible for industrial strife and a surly attitude to customers.

The future demands a co-operative culture of continuous improvement and innovation. In the future communications culture, each individual or work group will recognise that they are in a customer–supplier relationship with each other. Every organisation is composed of a series of work groups or teams working in processes which form interconnecting chains in many directions. Each process has a customer and a supplier, most of which are internal. Four-way communication becomes natural when each of these individuals or teams communicates with their own customers and suppliers. As open and frank communication becomes the norm, a new level of co-operation is created which can release the potential of everyone in the organisation.

The chasm between the two cultures is enormous, and change will not be achieved by executive decree or some form of motivational exercise. Management has to understand the concept of work processes and the change required in its own behaviour. The TQM process has to cascade this new comprehension down through the management levels. This is achieved by education, training and new work practices based on an understanding of the issues involved in improving work processes. Let us look now at some of the differences between small and large companies and see how these affect the approach to TQM.

Small Companies

The UK Department of Trade and Industry (DTI) defines small and medium companies as those with under 500 employees. It also notes that forty-five per cent of people employed in the manufacturing sector in Britain work for firms with fewer than 200 employees. If British manufacturing industry is to survive the fierce competition of the nineties, small companies *must* be involved in the quality revolution. How do small companies differ in organisation and culture from their larger brethren?

The obvious organisational difference is the flat management pyramid in small businesses. There are very few hierarchical levels to hinder communication. The managing director will probably only have one, or at most two, managerial levels between himself and the workforce. People within the company can relate to each other and their communication is simple and direct. Short lines of communication also bring short lines of commitment. Small companies need a unified approach (large companies can take differing approaches in each division), but this is usually a natural result of their unity of commitment. The managing director is in a position to say, 'This is the kind of company I want,' and expect it to happen – quickly.

However, in this communication strength there is, paradoxically, a weakness. The chief executive nearly always uses the personal pronoun 'I'; rarely 'we'. This attitude derives from the background of the 'boss': he is usually the founder or major shareholder of the firm or a member of the founding family. He will often be referred to by the employees by his first name – 'Mr John' – to differentiate him from other members of the family who may also work in the firm or were original founders. Ownership is the issue. Occasionally, the boss will be an outsider brought in by the family to 'stir things up a bit'. But he will still be 'owned' by the family, or at least that is how the employees will see his position. This can work against real teamwork.

This type of company will often be permeated with traditional or conventional wisdom. A typical phrase heard in this kind of organisation is, 'It was good enough for Mr Jacob, and it should be good enough for you.' This environment is not exactly designed to encourage change or teamwork.

However, it would be very unfair to stereotype all small companies in this way. Even companies run by a 'Mr John'. At their heart the majority of small companies are entrepreneurial; that's how they came to exist in the first place. They can be exciting and fun to work in; everyone is closer to the customer and to the results of his labour. From the quality management aspect the small company can bring about change more quickly. It is easier to get the TQM ball rolling.

The attitude and style of a manager in a small company will be significantly different from those of his counterpart in a large company. One reason for the differences lies in his promotion prospects. Unlike the large-company manager, he will spend little or no time considering how to get himself promoted out of his current job; his promotion prospects are few. But he feels secure, for he is unlikely to face outside competition, unless there is a rapid expansion of the business or other technical skills are required. He will generally find satisfaction in his work because his span of control is wider and he feels he has influence over a large proportion of the company's activities.

The number and breadth of functional operations managed by a single individual in a small firm would require a number of specialist managers in a large company. Quite apart from the scarcity of other managers at his own level, the small-company boss has few to whom he can delegate less important issues. This makes it very difficult to organise priorities for his own time or attention. His job is complex and requires a wide range of skills. However, he has little time for personal development and acquiring higher communication and team-building skills. He needs another meeting 'like a hole in the head'. Even though he may appreciate the need for quality improvement, he may wonder where he is ever going to find the time to do something about it.

Another facet of the small company which directly relates to the need for TQM is the strong customer orientation of the managers. This is what TQM teaches, but unfortunately in the small company this attitude tends to lead to a 'fix it' mentality rather than a 'get to the root cause' approach. The manager reacts strongly to complaints from a customer because he really sees it as a matter of survival (he doesn't have all that many customers) and to some extent because he views customer relations as his great strength versus the larger competition. There is nothing wrong with his reaction, but the other factors in his management style give him little time for investigating causes or initial preventive planning. He spends a large part of his time firefighting, and indeed probably views this as the main role of the manager. On the other hand, despite the lack of planning, the objectives of the small company are usually clear and straightforward.

The need for small and medium-sized companies to join the road to continuous improvement is no less than for large companies. They face the same competitive pressures from the changing perceptions of customers and if they don't respond to them, other small companies will. However, few have the knowledge, the time or the staff to implement the improvement process. This means outside help. Few feel that they have the money to employ the best consultants and so often make do with one-day seminars or incompetent consultants (NOTE: the most expensive consultants are not always the best consultants!) In this situation there is a need for co-operative ventures.

Most small companies are surrounded by others in a similar position regarding quality. They are often grouped on an industrial estate or in a business park. In any case groupings can be organised within a relatively small area. Managers from a number of companies can get together at breakfast or evening meetings for seminars, training sessions and the sharing of ideas and experiences. In this way the companies could club together and afford any consultant and educational services they needed. There can be some resistance to sharing information about product defects and organisational problems, but as individual managers get to know each other they soon realise that they have similar problems.

In Britain the DTI, in the eighties, has assisted companies with under 500 employees by paying part of the consultant fees (under certain conditions) to assist with assessments and certification to the UK quality systems standard. If government or local authorities want to assist further, they could promote the establishment of *quality clubs* along the lines suggested here.

Large Companies

The most important fact about large companies is that they are *large*. This fact alone shapes the management culture and the attitudes of all employees. Organising meaningful communication throughout the organisation is a headache. Most employees are remote from both the leadership of the company and from the external customer. These issues have to be addressed in a strategy for the successful implementation of TQM.

The idea that large is beautiful was prevalent in the sixties and seventies. The era of short-term financial management encouraged the moves towards 'economies of scale' and centrally controlled decision making. Huge central bureaucracies of 'bean counters' and planning staff frustrated middle operational management. Top management lost touch with the real problems (and the customers) and, in so doing, lost the loyalty of middle management. Major corporations were becoming too centralised to survive in a world of dynamic change.

The cold wind of economic change, in the late seventies, exposed many of the dinosaurs. The large companies resorted to heavy pruning and made a conscious effort to devolve decision making. These management actions have been relatively successful; British Steel and ICI are shining examples. However, cultures are not changed overnight. Despite a severe shock to the whole system, vestiges of the original culture and attitudes remain. The difference today is that senior management recognises the situation and wants to change. TQM is seen by many as a form of umbrella under which to accomplish this change.

Large companies are good examples of the present culture pyramid illustrated in Figure 25 earlier in this chapter. They have substantial departmental hierarchies: vertical chains of command and communication down through one function. Departmental fortresses are created (see Figure 26) and defended against perceived attacks from other fortresses.

Managers are proud to state, 'I stand up for my own people.' Communication is usually top-down, occasionally bottom-up and very rarely sideways. Each department works in isolation. All its people are working hard and well to produce results to the high standards defined *within* the castle moat. These standards have little reference to the requirements of the user of what they produce. When they are finished the results are thrown over the wall to the next fortress. The real results are endless changes notices; designs that take little account of manufacturing practices; materials that meet the financial requirements of purchasing but little else – overall, endless hassle and pointing of fingers.

The over-the-wall syndrome bedevils quality. The job of the TQM process is to open some doors in the walls. Once the doors are open and the defenders venture outside they gradually come to like the freedom and open communication. They eventually realise that the walls were pointless and send for Joshua and his trumpets.

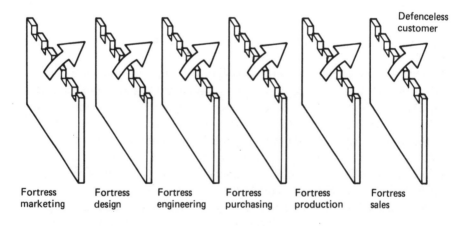

Figure 26 *Fortress mentality and the over-the-wall syndrome.*

The fortress mentality found in many large companies engenders attitudes which can provide obstacles to TQM. Managers are highly politicised, watching for the winds of change or flavour of the month from on high. They can leap onto the quality bandwagon, but leap off equally quickly if their antennae detect a shift in the wind. This attitude means that senior management's observable continuous commitment to the improvement process is vitally important. They must maintain the constancy of purpose. Again, departmental managers with the fortress viewpoint will avoid risk at all costs, and as a corollary rarely tell their own managers what they really think about any situation. They want to see 'which way the wind is blowing' before declaring their position. Completely contrary to the position in the small company is the difficulty of persuading such managers that they should enlarge their sphere of interest – that they should make a conscious effort to understand the problems and requirements of a manager in another fortress.

However, large companies do have major advantages when it comes to implementing TQM. They generally have the resources of both people and money. Within the organisation is a high level of specialist skills which can be utilised as the TQM process proceeds. More data and knowledge is available, and planning is in the nature of the organisation. Perhaps the greatest advantage is that if the company can accomplish the necessary cultural change a vast reservoir of talent, energy and enthusiasm is there to be unlocked. The heady air outside the fortress walls can invigorate far more than just communication – *Kaizen* will be blowing through the organisation.

The TQM strategy for a large company can be developed either for the organisation as a whole or 'bite by bite' across the organisation. The current mood favours autonomously managed individual profit centres within the corporation. Many large companies today are effectively operating as a group of small and medium-sized companies. In the devolved corporation the subsidiary managing directors or the divisional general managers may attend the executive awareness sessions. After that they develop individual assessments and strategies. Alternatively, separate divisions or subsidiaries start the whole process of TQM on their own initiative. The organisation issues for both the centralised and the devolved approach are discussed in detail in Chapter 27.

25 *Not invented here*

The culture of an organisation has taken time to form. It is based on its history, its beliefs, and above all, its people. An attempt to change the culture requires careful consideration. Hence the argument for careful assessment of the present culture and of the agents for change. One part of the decision to change is the choice between using internal resources alone, or involving outside assistance. Be careful in whom you put your trust; this is your culture, not the consultant's.

There are two principal reasons for rejecting the 'go it alone' approach. The first is based upon internal attitudes within the company and the second is based on time considerations. Let us look at each of these factors in turn.

There are many vested interests within companies, particularly large corporations, which will resist outside help. Each company has its own epithets for outside consultants. Some are valid, some are nonsensical. The former must be taken into account when selecting a consultant. When a company is considering the internal approach to changing the way it operates, it should ask, 'How did we get here in the first place?' By relying on internal management decisions? Internal advice is not necessarily the best.

Many inside the organisation will resist outside help on the basis that the outsider does not understand the business. To some extent this is true. The insider does have the advantage that he knows the corporate language and can see the political and economic implications of each step in the improvement process. On the other hand, the insider probably does not have the knowledge or credibility to effect change on his own.

Education is an essential element of the strategy for TQM. Probably the biggest danger is to ask the in-house training department to develop the educational programme. Almost without exception they will mix partly understood concepts with a set of their own prejudices or departmental ambitions. They can end up confusing everybody, including themselves. For example, the author has seen the concept of zero defects linked with a no-blame ethos to become 'that's close enough'. But equally important is the credibility of a third party. The outside consultant is more likely to be accepted and attention given to his arguments and opinions. After all, the internal training department is, understandably, perceived by the workforce as part of the present culture.

The second principal reason for rejecting the internal approach is the time it takes. First of all, there are unlikely to be many people within the organisation who have sufficient knowledge of TQM concepts, and even fewer who will have practical experience of implementing TQM. An outsider with the requisite knowledge and experience could be recruited to head the process as a TQM co-ordinator. However, by definition these are rare animals, certainly in Europe. The best consultant companies in this field spend some six months training their consultants before releasing them on clients – and they have usually had experience before joining the consultant firm.

The company will have to take time and effort to gain the requisite knowledge and select the appropriate approach. Time visiting other companies, touring the world to gain experience, attending seminars and reading the textbooks. The individuals selected to carry out this task then have to train other facilitators, develop educational programmes and then implement the improvement process. All of this will have taken up to four years. And the company has to wait a long time before it can be certain that the individuals properly understood the concepts and were capable of transferring that knowledge to others in the company. It has been calculated that it will take the West up to ten years just to get where the Japanese are now – and they are not standing still. No, if you have perceived the need there is no time to be lost.

Choosing a consultant

There are various types of consultant and they have various approaches to TQM. Several consultant firms specialise in quality management and some of the large generalist consultants are active in this area. A few major corporations who have been very successful in implementing TQM have established their own 'quality institutes' and are prepared to act as consultants to other firms. This is particularly so in the United States. The smaller company may find that their trade or professional associations are capable of advising them, and several universities and business colleges are able to help with awareness or educational pro-grammes. A large company may use more than one consultant as they progress and identify different kinds of specialist assistance they need.

The type or types of consultant being considered should be evaluated in relation to the company's position along the road to continuous improvement. A way to assess the company's position is to compare it with the six stages of quality improvement (see Chapter 5). When assessing the position in this way, look carefully at differences between locations or functions. Manufacturing may well be a lot further down the road than other operations. In this situation, one consultant may be selected to assist with the overall cultural change and another to install sophisticated statistical tools.

The advantages of good external consultants are that they are independent of the organisation, they know what they are doing and they can achieve credibility within the organisation. After all, they live by their reputation. In summary, they bring:

- independent judgement
- no individual bias towards elements of the organisation
- ability to cross the hidden barriers in communication
- freedom from company prejudices or enthusiasms
- absence of real or perceived self-interest
- knowledge and experience.

Working with a consultant on changing the culture of the organisation is not the same as working with a technical specialist. It should be an ongoing partnership of interest in your success. This cultural aspect of the relationship with the consultant was discussed in Chapter 5 and illustrated in Figures 5 and 6. Before selecting your consultant, discuss the situation in depth. Ensure that he fully understands the cultural history of the company and will be prepared to work to the company mission and its declared policies for quality. The consultant may well be able to advise on the development of the policies, principles and values which will impart the needed constancy of purpose to the process.

The dangers of relying on the internal development of educational materials were pointed out earlier. However, there are also dangers with externally developed educational programmes. Some are packaged and make little allowance for the specific industry or culture of the receiving students. This can hinder communication. Discuss this with the consultant and examine his educational materials. In the assessment and planning phase the consultant should work with the client to develop the materials. The client's own policies, principles and organisation should be included as an integral part of the educational material. Additionally, industry-specific examples and use of the company logo will provide identity and greatly aid communication throughout the organisation.

Companies and consultants working together towards the same goals can transform the corporate culture beyond most expectations.

26 *This is where we are going!*

At the end of Chatper 23 our Quality Steering Committee had concluded their initial assessment. They had also defined some further data they required to complete the assessment. The provision of these data may require detailed surveys of employee attitudes and market research into the company's competitive position. A prime requirement, if it did not already exist, was a survey of customer perceptions of the company. Assuming that the facts are all in, the committee now have sufficient comprehension to commit themselves to a strategy for the implementation of TQM.

In real life, depending on the size of the organisation, the development of the strategy and a detailed business plan for quality improvement may take several weeks. It will involve the QSC members, but a lot of the detailed planning will be done by the TQM co-ordinator and his facilitators (their role will be explained later in this chapter) in concert with the consultants.

At this stage the QSC will confine its deliberations to the broad strategy. The consultant will introduce the key elements and the group will work together to provide the basis for further action. Primarily they are concerned with the quality improvement process organisation and the educational requirements. This will establish the committee and process team membership and structure. It will also define the number of people to be educated in each category over a time period.

The data from this broad strategy session will enable the consultant to prepare a full proposal for consideration by the chief executive and/or the QSC. This proposal will define the broad education and training course schedule and the level of consultant support required. The financial investment to meet the strategy will also be defined. Even though the consultant has been working with senior management for several days (for which he will have charged fees) it is recommended that no final commitment be given to the consultant until after this stage.

The proposal will indicate the degree to which the consultant has understood the culture and nature of the business. The senior executives will have to judge whether the consultant's proposal meets the requirements of the business. The consultant's overall approach may fully meet the approval of the executives, but individuals from the consultant company may not fit the chemistry of the company or be unacceptable for other reasons. This issue must be discussed with a senior executive from the consultant firm and resolved before going ahead. Some consultant staff might be excellent conceptual thinkers and good at developing strategies, but hopeless at teaching senior management. This may all sound ultra-conservative, but this early planning process is absolutely vital. The company *only has one chance to get the process right*. Try launching a quality improvement process two years after the first attempt has failed!

The Quality Business Plan

Now that the consultant has been selected, work can start on preparing the *quality business plan*. This should be developed in partnership with the consultant, and should include the following elements:

- The strategic direction or *quality mission* of the organisation.
- The *quality policy* to be adopted by the organisation.
- The *principles* and *values* which will be shared by the whole organisation.
- The *organisation* of the process.
- The *education plan* to involve every employee.
- The *strategies* and *tactics* for implementation of the process.
- The *resources* required to implement the plan.
- The *quality goals* and *criteria* for measurement.

We will examine each of these points in detail, but first two questions must be answered:

1 *Why is a Quality Business Plan needed?* Present company culture in the West is dominated by the business objectives of cost and schedule. Quality is compromised in the struggle to achieve these two objectives. The decision has been made to change the priorities and make quality 'first among equals' along with cost and schedules. Quality and business are no longer separate issues. Quality and business are one and indivisible.

Quality will not happen just because the executives state that it has to happen. Management must cause quality to happen. An effective Business Plan provides a clear view of the road ahead. It defines the destination, the principles, the strategies and the organisation needed to complete the journey. It establishes a stable base to ensure that the journey can be controlled and kept on course. It provides firm guidelines for those charged with implementation. It is the first stage in commitment and communication.

2 *Who will help develop the Plan?* During the development of the broad strategy an organisation was structured to implement the process. This organisation is planned to fit the structure and nature of the business. It is to include a number of process teams (TQM teams) and task forces. During the proposal discussions the consultant and the chief executive (supported by the TQM co-ordinator) will have broadly defined the membership of these teams. A member of each team will be selected, at this stage, to be the 'quality champion' for that location or function of the company.

These individuals will be *facilitators* assisting the teams to implement the process of change. These facilitators will need specialist education at the commencement of the planning phase (the nature of this education is described later). The facilitators will work closely with the TQM co-ordinator and the consultant to develop the detailed plan for submission to the QSC.

The remainder of this chapter examines the main elements of the Quality Business Plan in order to explain more fully what each part includes and how they relate to each other.

The Quality Mission: In reality there should be no such thing as a separate and distinct 'Quality Mission'. The words have been used to emphasise a point. There should be a *company* mission which embraces quality and from which it is inseparable. The mission is the purpose of the company's existence. The mission is usually changed only when the organisation decides to pursue a completely new market, or the same market in a completely different way. It could be argued that the way the mission is carried out is more properly contained within the operating principles. The point to be made is that quality is now an integral part of the business objectives. A company mission must be stated. If the mission is already clearly defined, the executives must consider whether it fully encompasses the new direction the company is envisaging. Should the mission be amended? Would the goal of putting quality before profit fit with the mission? The company mission, equated with the thrust towards quality, must be included in the Quality Business Plan.

The Quality Policy: This must be developed by the executives and promulgated throughout the company. In a large company it may be appropriate to develop divisional or subsidiary quality policies. They commit that operation and have more relevance to the people involved. However, these divisional policies must be complementary to, and in no way conflict with, the corporate policy. There are many examples of quality policies but the main point is that the one a company adopts must be *that organisation's own policy*. Do not import a policy from another company or your consultant. The executives should by all means examine other policies, but should develop a policy of their own to which they are happy to commit themselves, and would be enthusiastically prepared to discuss with any employee. One word of warning: do not use subjective or ambiguous clauses. There can be no compromise with quality.

Principles and Values: These create the environment in which everyone in the company will be enabled to work together to meet the company mission and the quality policy. In short, they are the company culture. The company has already decided to change its culture; therefore it probably will need to add to and amend the existing principles and values. The executives should examine these from the standpoint of a culture designed continuously to delight the customer and continuously to seek improvement.

A set of principles and values to meet the TQM culture was discussed in Chapter 11. It can be used as a guide, but it is important that the leadership of the company develop principles for their own organisation. However, it is imperative that these state how the company will act towards its customers, its suppliers and its employees. They should also state how the company expects its employees to act towards each other, and particularly how it expects its management to act. In today's business environment the principles and values of a company should also express its responsibility to the community at large, and in the case of a public company its responsibility to the shareholders.

The company mission, the quality policy and the principles and values, once determined, should be included as an integral part of the quality awareness and educational material.

Organisation: The organisational strategy for TQM will depend on the size, structure and nature of the business. But before the strategy is developed, one important principle must be understood. The TQM organisation is not responsible for quality or quality improvement. It is responsible for managing a facilitative process – a process that will assist managers and people to take ownership of quality; a process in which the concept of improvement will become ingrained in each individual. The TQM process manages the provision of education, systems and tools so that all can take responsibility for quality.

The TQM process starts with senior management and is cascaded down the organisation. The Quality Steering Committee in our hypothetical example was formed to focus senior management's attention on the development of a strategy and detailed plans for the implementation of the process. In a small company this may be the full extent of the TQM process organisation. In that case the QSC would then implement and monitor their own plans. However, in larger companies the complexity of the organisation will require a different approach. A TQM process organisation will have to be established to assist the QSC in the execution of its plans.

The organisational process starts with the appointment of the TQM co-ordinator. He is the executive who will manage the process, and he is responsible to the QSC for its success. The post requires the same level of authority and influence as that of the other senior operational directors. In the majority of cases this will be a full-time appointment. The title used for this position should fit the culture of the company, but should be distinctive from the existing quality operations. Vice President or Director of Quality Management are typical titles.

The central organisation for TQM (see Figure 27) should be kept as small as possible. Any tendency to create a quality management empire should be resisted. In any case line management would resist such a tendency, either throttling the TQM process or, equally dangerous, delegating quality management issues to the new organisation. The leaders or beacons of quality must work through the normal line organisation.

The ideal approach is for the co-ordinator to have a small secretariat. From time to time, a number of specialists could be seconded to the

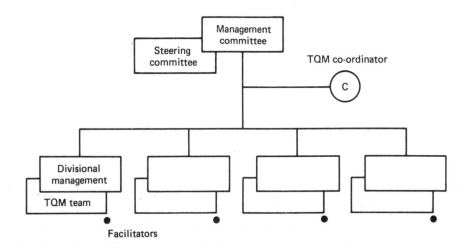

Figure 27 *The TQM organisation – shadow committees, TQM co-ordinator and facilitators.*

quality secretariat on an ad hoc basis as needed. The facilitators and others assisting the co-ordinator should generally retain their normal direct-reporting lines within divisions, locations or functional departments of the company. In that situation they would have a dotted line responsibility, via the TQM team organisation, to the co-ordinator. The teams themselves are essentially the normal management teams meeting separately to focus on quality. They are not a separate organisation responsibility for quality.

The process of change will be cascaded down the organisation and managed through the TQM teams. These teams will organise the process in specific locations or other groupings determined by the company structure. They will be composed of the senior functional management at each location. In addition to the TQM teams a number of specialist *task forces* will be formed, usually for a limited period until the task has been completed. A typical task would be to develop a Corrective Action System to be used across the company. These teams are part of the facilitative or TQM process (see Figure 28).

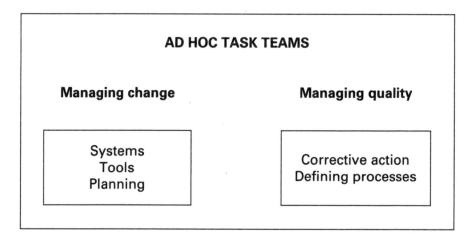

Figure 28   *The TQM organisation does not manage quality – that is the job of line management.*

Specialist *work process teams* will also be formed on a similar basis to the task forces. Their task will be to analyse the key process flows across the company. The composition and principle terms of reference of all these teams and task forces are developed in Chapter 27. These teams, like the corrective action and problem solving teams, are part of the process in action rather than being facilitative. They will be established by line management as a necessary adjunct to their improvement activities. The TQM organisation may assist in their establishment and training, but not in their management. The TQM teams will, however, see that they are being established in all relevant groups.

The Business Plan will define the shape of the organisation and the number of teams and task forces required to suit the company structure and number of employees. This in turn will help establish the type and amount of education required to meet the TQM objectives.

Education: The education plan is the heart of the TQM process. This part of the Business Plan must define the curricula and broad schedule of education and training required at each level of the organisation.

Every individual in the company will eventually be educated so that they fully understand the need for change and their part in the improvement process. The aim is to develop a common language of quality and inculcate shared values and principles (see Figure 29). The perception of need and the ability to absorb new concepts (or, perhaps, trust management commitment) will differ at each level, but the result must be a common commitment to continuous improvement.

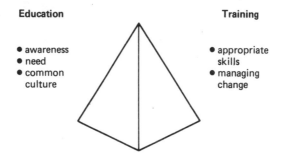

Figure 29 *The role of education and training in the TQM process.*

The training aspect of the plan is directed specifically at the individual's role in the company or in the management of the TQM process. Most courses will contain both education and training elements. The whole education plan will extend over a long period, its exact length depending on the numbers to be educated and the pace which the QSC believes is right for the company.

The planning schedule (the example shows one used by Resource Evaluation Limited, quality management consultants) breaks down into a number of phases:

- Phase One provides the executives and facilitators with sufficient knowledge and commitment to plan the improvement process. This

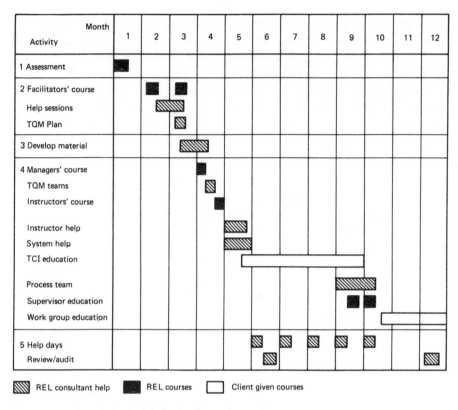

Figure 30   *A typical schedule for implementing action.*

will comprise executive workshops and facilitator's courses and workshops.

- Phase Two involves preparations for implementation. Members of the TQM teams and task forces will attend process management courses. Effectively this is a substantial nucleus of senior and middle management. The numbers involved at this stage are largely determined by the locational organisational structure discussed earlier. The courses will include the key elements of the Business Plan and the policy and principles developed by the QSC.

- Phase Three deals with preparations for general education. A number of in-house instructors will have been selected to teach the TCI course. This course is the central core of the company-wide education process. All managers, supervisors and specialist workers (eg, engineers, software experts etc) will attend a series of weekly two-hour sessions. Communication will be strengthened if the instructors are drawn from management rather than the training groups. This is not usually a full-time role; instructors could teach one or two sessions per week. The objective of this course is to equip people to manage quality in their day-to-day operations. Executives and facilitators should also attend the TCI course; their original courses equipped them to manage the process – not quality.

- Phase Four can be summed up as 'educating the people'. Management is now in a position to manage quality and to respond to initiatives from either shop floor or administrative workers. At this stage the final phase of education can begin. This will generally be given by supervisors, who must have completed the TCI education. Short workshops will prepare supervisors for this role. Phase Four may begin between six to nine months after the start of the process, depending on the size of the company.

- Phase Five may be described as the continuous development phase. This educational phase will continue for ever as a programme of continuous development of everyone in the company. It may well start before the final phase of the basic education has been completed. Courses on the use of analytical and statistical methods and general courses on problem solving and management development, etc, are normal aspects of this phase.

The education plan explained in these pages represents the authors' view of the requirements. Other consultants may differ in the content and extent of the education they recommend for the implementation of TQM. However, in general they will follow a similar pattern. The essential ingredient, in our view, is that every one of these courses and the whole education plan must be tailored to fit the specific company. To do otherwise, or to accept unadapted packaged education, will impair the effectiveness of the educational process. The curricula for these proposed courses will be developed in Chapter 29 'Back to School'.

Strategies and Tactics: When the initial Business Plan is developed there may not be enough knowledge of implementation within the company to include a section on strategies and tactics. However, the quality secretariat and the locational TQM teams will quickly develop strategies and tactics for the implementation of the improvement process throughout the company. These should be added to the Business Plan at appropriate review periods by the QSC. They will act as a useful monitoring aid to ensure that the focus on team action is maintained; a number of them, such as awareness, improvement suggestions, goal setting and the general use or measurement, will be discussed later.

Resources: A principal role of management is to ensure that the resoures required at each stage of the improvement process are provided and properly utilised. They must, therefore, be fully identified in the Business Plan. They will include money and time: money for external

assistance, education and printing, etc, and time provision for individuals at each level of the organisation. An area for very clear definition
is which resources are to be supplied centrally and which are to be
provided from departmental operating budgets. The financial control
system of the company may make it difficult for individual managers to
seek consultant assistance when needed if the resource has not been
provided for in the Business Plan budgeting process.

Quality Goals and Criteria: This chapter has concentrated on the development of the Quality Business Plan. However, this should be viewed as an
integral part of the overall corporate business plan, which will have
established general business objectives and performance goals. Quality
goals and criteria should be closely linked to these overall business goals
in any assessment of the company's present position. This process may
result in some amendment of the original business goals.

Two types of performance goals should be established in the initial
phases of quality improvement. These can be defined as those designed
to improve the quality performance of the company and those designed
to measure how well implementation of the improvement process is
proceeding.

Quality performance goals should be quantitative and could relate to
the reduction of the cost of quality at stated periods, defect level rates
and other ratios. Many of these specific performance-related areas will
have been discovered at the assessment period.

Qualitative and quantitative criteria for measuring the success of
implementation will derive from the implementation plan. The criteria
would include goals for the completion of the educational phases and
periodic surveys of employee attitudes. They *must* include clearly
defined locational goals for the implementation of the systems for quality
improvement. The establishment and use of the corrective action system
and the departmental implementation of measurement are typical of
such goals.

Before we leave the subject of quality measurement, a word of caution
about the 'Cost of Quality' criterion is in order. Many quality gurus and
consultants select the Cost of Quality as the basis for measuring quality
improvement. Indeed, Philip Crosby elevates Cost of Quality to an
'Absolute', as *the* measurement criterion for the improvement process.
The authors have considerable doubts about this concept, regarding
both theory and practical application.

When the ultimate aim of quality control or management was the
elimination of defects as against defined requirements, the theory was
tenable. However, that is not the ultimate aim of TQM. The elimination
of error is only a stage on the road to sustained competitive advantage.
Cost of Quality is by no means a complete measure of a company's and

its people's commitment to continuous improvement, although it can be used as one of a group of quality performance goals. Cost of Quality, or more precisely the price of non-conformance, is a powerful tool for initially focusing management attention on the need to change and for establishing priorities for corrective action.

The danger of using Cost of Quality as the primary measurement system can be seen in the lengths some companies go to in implementing the system. The time and effort expended in establishing the system and collecting the data would have been better used in analysing and improving work processes. Managers become adroit at massaging the system when it is used as a form of budgetary or operational control. In the authors' experience it tends to reinforce the vertical measurement of people by numerate results, rather than concentrating attention on the processes.

The Completed Plan: Starting a New Way of Life

The company Business Plan now incorporates a planned approach to quality improvement. Henceforth, every Business Plan prepared in the company will include the actions and goals associated with quality as a way of business life. Having carefully planned the implementation of TQM, it is now up to the management of the company to *make it happen*.

27 Making it happen

TQM in itself is not a fixed goal but rather a process to manage the change or delta between the company's present culture and a culture dedicated to total and continuous improvement. TQM will often be up against a strongly entrenched culture, particularly in a large organisation. The existing culture can slowly strangle the whole process if management does not maintain a constancy of purpose. Certainly many quality improvement processes never really get off the ground, or disappear after initial enthusiasm wears off.

Lack of management commitment is usually blamed for failure to meet the original expectations, but this is an overly simplistic explanation. Changing management and employee behaviour and attitudes within an organisation is a difficult process. Change never comes easily and it will not happen just because the chief executive is committed to a new approach. In the authors' opinion the reason for failure more usually lies with the initial approach to implementation, in other words the way management tries to make the change happen.

Management can gain some comprehension of the extent of failings in a company from the initial assessment described in Chapter 23. This is likely to bring about a strong commitment to change. However, this new commitment can sometimes lead to over-enthusiasm for immediate action. Some executives are tempted to completely re-organise the company to meet the quality challenge. In addition, every weapon in the armoury of TQM is deployed immediately. But too much change, implemented too quickly will cause serious indigestion. Line management still has to manage the business. If disruption is caused by the implementation of TQM the process will be resisted by middle management.

Another temptation for executives is to set up a separate organisation for quality improvement. Nearly every book or course on quality management describes organisations liberally packed with quality improvement and corrective action teams or some similarly-titled groups. These are often misunderstood by executives as being separate from normal line management. As a result they establish a new bureaucracy which soon becomes institutionalised. Line management now has no need to change, because a new fortress has been established; quality can be 'thrown over the wall' to the new teams.

Nevertheless, cultural change will require that action be taken and that an organisational structure be established. To prevent the problems discussed above, the organisational structure for quality should be married to the existing management structure. In addition, the quality action plans will define a specific stage (described later) for transferring ownership of the TQM process to line management.

The process of change will be better understood when realisation grows that although the present culture was not achieved by careful planning, neither did it happen by accident. It has been created steadily over time by the way things are done in the company: by the way objectives are set, by the way people are measured, by the way functional or departmental specialisations have grown – by force of habit. The culture will be changed in a similar way; that is by steadily doing things differently. This process can be likened to adult learning. The change will be achieved more quickly than it took the present culture to emerge, because knowledge now allows the actions to be planned to ensure that things *are* done differently.

Union Involvement

Before the structure and actions for TQM can be developed, there is an important element of attitudinal change that must be addressed. A major concern of many organisations is how the unions will react and when, or if, they should be involved in the quality improvement process.

The relationship between management, employees and trade unions in the development of company cultures was noted in Chapter 7. In general those comments applied to industrial growth in most nations. Unions represented workers, trades and even middle management with the objective of getting the best deal possible from the owners or executives of both single organisations and whole sections of industry. Many industrial disputes were long and bitter feuds which left a residue of controversy and confrontation. However, many unions developed a real interest in the success of the business employing their members, and this allowed reasonable negotiation.

Non-British readers may not realise that the social and political history of Britain led to a different evolution of trade unions. The Labour Party (socialist in its ideology) grew from the trade union movement and represented the political ambitions of the working class. Though weakening, this position persists and the unions are still the main paymasters of one of the UK's two major political parties. This has meant that trade union leaders in Britain have external political objectives in a trade dispute. In other words, many industrial disputes have been politically rather than economically motivated. This history has established a very strong 'them and us' attitude in British industry and public service organisations.

Management cannot be absolved from blame for the growth of adversarial relations in industry. Their own attitudes often fostered the 'class war' mentality or provided emotional issues for politically-motivated union leaders to exploit. In many cases line management abdicated their responsibility for industrial relations either to personnel departments or, at a higher level, to governments. Since the advent of Margaret Thatcher, new legislation, the growth of white collar industries and the more materialistic aspirations of workers have modified these attitudes. However, old suspicions die hard and the 'them and us' syndrome is still a major problem in British business. Union attitudes and communication with organised labour are crucial issues in effecting cultural change in Britain. For those organisations with a strong union presence, the involvement of the unions in the process of quality improvement is an essential factor in TQM planning.

Unions must be involved early in the process. Delay will only foster suspicion that management are 'up to something'. Rumour in business usually has a tendency to be negative. Quality improvement can be represented as getting the workers to do more for less or as another cost-cutting exercise. Union comprehension of the issues will remove these suspicions and pave the way for close co-operation. After all, the cry from the shop floor has always been, 'When will management get its act together?' The initial stages of TQM are designed to do just that, and if this is clearly understood a new era of labour-management collaboration can begin.

Union representatives must be involved in awareness sessions at the planning stage. Choice of these representatives will depend on the size of the company and the nature of union representation. Unions have their own management structure, and their awareness and education must mirror the 'cascade' approach within the company. This relates to both timing and content. In many cases more than one union may be involved, and all should be treated in a similar manner. The real influence on internal union representatives or the workers themselves may lie outside the boundaries of the company in local or national union managements. These are essential issues to be considered at early meetings of the Quality Steering Committee.

The Structure for Total Quality Management

There are two factors to bear in mind when designing the structure for TQM and planning initial actions:

1 The TQM organisational structure should mirror and not supplant the existing organisation.
2 TQM actions are distinct from improvement actions. All TQM actions are facilitative; they are designed to assist the normal organisation in taking improvement actions.

Everyone, management and people, will carry out their duties in a different way according to their personal role. The cumulative effect of these differences will result in a new culture of total continuous improvement.

Steering committees are formed at the apex of cross-functional management of a distinct quality improvement process. For example, in a large corporation steering committees could be established at divisional management level. In the majority of cases the steering committee is likely to be the board or management committee of the company.

TQM teams should be established at the highest level of cross-functional management in a specific location of the business. A very large site may require TQM teams dedicated to functions or business units. A dispersed organisation of small locations (such as a car hire firm) may be better suited to TQM teams at area or regional levels. Some of these issues were discussed in Chapter 24.

The last chapter described the essential shadow nature of the steering committee and the TQM teams. This fact alone indicates that the TQM structure should follow as closely as possible the natural management structure of the organisation. The launch of the TQM process is not the moment to redefine the company organisation. The activities of work process improvement may well in itself raise questions as to the efficacy of the existing organisation, and indeed some reorganisation may result from specific improvement goals. However, this is a much later stage in the process of managing change.

TQM Actions

The initial TQM actions were described in the last chapter. These included the establishment of the steering committee, the selection and training of the TQM co-ordinator and TQM team facilitators, and above all the development of the Quality Business Plan. Figure 31 shows the

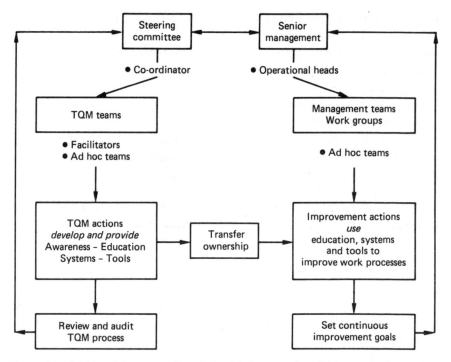

Figure 31 *Making it happen – the relationship between the TQM organisation and the management organisation.*

distict role of the TQM teams and permanent management teams in implementing TQM actions and improvement actions.

The implementation of the Plan starts with the TQM actions. The key actions can be summarised as follows:

1 Form TQM teams and train members.
2 Initiate company-wide awareness of TQM.
3 Train the instructors.
4 Implement the education element of the Business Plan, starting with senior management and cascading down the organisation.
5 Develop TQM systems for corrective action, recognition and improvement suggestions.
6 Develop TQM tools or documentation for work process analysis, requirements and measurement.
7 Establish review procedures.

These actions are not necessarily taken in a strict sequential order. Many will start at the same time and involve separate ad hoc teams. In the following pages we offer some guidelines for each of the seven key actions and point out some of the pitfalls to be avoided.

1 *Form TQM teams.* As described earlier, the teams will usually consist of the management of the location or area as defined in the Plan. The facilitator is a member of the team and may also have been selected from the management group.

We have seen the role of the facilitators in developing the Plan. The facilitator's role in the team is to act as TQM specialist and liaison with other teams. Facilitators may also take a direct role in the education process by acting as instructors on internal courses. Clearly they must be well-organised individuals with good communication skills. This is a magnificent opportunity to develop potential high flyers within the organisation. They will learn a great deal about the company, broaden their perspective and become quality leaders.

Team members must not just rely on the newly developed specialist knowledge of the facilitator. They need education in the TQM process. This management education will include all the elements of the company's Business Plan for quality which the team will be helping to implement.

The team's first tasks are to select a chairman and agree the terms of reference under which it will operate. These should include a clear statement of purpose and of the team's responsibilities. It is important that the frequency and duration of meetings should be set from the outset. All the managers involved have a heavy workload and, to put it mildly, do not welcome additional meetings. A sensible approach is to hold TQM team and steering committee meetings on the same day as the regular management meetings. However, they should always precede the management meetings. This is to avoid quality being discussed in the confrontational atmosphere which can sometimes be fostered during discussions of other management issues. TQM meetings should be limited to one hour or a period agreed in advance by all attendees. Remember, these teams are the management group meeting separately to focus their attention on TQM. Organising TQM team meetings in this way will help to overcome the natural resistance to more meetings and help individual members to plan their input. The facilitator and chairman should ensure that each meeting works to a prepared agenda and that clear and concise minutes of agreed actions are distributed before the next meeting.

2 *Initiate company-wide awareness.* The two classic errors made in trying to promote a company-wide awareness of the commitment to TQM are to do it too early or to do it too late. Executives are often tempted to demonstrate their commitment by making speeches or placing

announcements in the company newspaper about quality and TQM immediately they have made the decision to go ahead. The problem at this stage is that few if any of the locational managers know what is being talked about and what is involved. It can easily be perceived as merely a new flavour of the month. These managers cannot become truly committed without comprehension of the need.

If the announcement of TQM is delayed too long, however, rumour will replace fact. Co-ordinators and facilitators have been selected. They have disappeared to courses and planning sessions. Management have been called to special meetings and consultants are around. There has been sufficient action to start discussion. If senior management keep silent, rumours will abound about mergers, acquisitions or a major cost-cutting exercise. Once the TQM teams have been established and the members educated, there is sufficient comprehension at locational level to promote company-wide awareness.

The form and extent of the awareness programme is a complex issue in itself. It requires careful planning to avoid the pitfalls which exist simply because of the differing perceptions of need at various levels of the company. This whole subject is discussed in more detail in Chapter 28, 'What's In It For Me?'

3 *Train internal instructors*. Education and training is key to the successful implementation of TQM. The Quality Business Plan will have defined the extent and the pace of education and training throughout the organisation. Irrespective of the education system selected, it will be more successful if courses are given by internal instructors – people who have knowledge of the organisation and will be around to answer queries. Ideally, the instructors chosen should be managers with some ability to communicate. Some instructors can be selected from the company training department, but on no account should the responsibility for training be given to that department. The dangers of this policy were discussed earlier. Line managers will have the respect and practical knowledge needed to carry out this responsibility. The number of instructors required is a function of the number of people to be trained, the full or part-time situation of instructors and the pace at which the company has decided to implement TQM.

The instructors will require training and practice-teaching sessions with the material they will use, as well as some basic training in the techniques of teaching. The type of preparation envisaged is described in Chapter 29, 'Back to School'. The instructors would require an intensive course of one week.

4 *Start implementing the education plan*. Approximately one month after the completion of instructor training the education plan should be commenced. The delay is to give the instructors more opportunity to

familiarise themselves with the material and to develop examples from company experience. An early improvement action is the establishment of ad hoc teams to analyse and define the flow of some key company processes. The scheduling, organisation and monitoring of TQM education and training in a large organisation is a major task and is the responsibility of the TQM team. This is one area where the experience of the training department can be helpful. The TQM instructors could form their own ad hoc committee to which a member of the training department could be seconded.

5 *Develop TQM systems.* As the process of TQM education proceeds, management and work groups will require systems to help them improve work processes, involve people in the improvement process and take specific corrective actions. Specifically, these systems will be the company systems for corrective action, formal recognition and suggestions. Each of these is described in later chapters, but it should be noted here that their development is an early responsibility of the TQM team. The development of a corrective action system is the first priority and can often be accomplished by the facilitators at the planning stage. The design of this system must be completed early, as it should form an integral part of the education material. All the systems will require that documents needed to use them be readily available to all employees at all locations. This is a responsibility of the TQM teams.

Generally, the best way to accomplish the development and provision of these systems is to set up small and short-term ad hoc teams chaired by members of the TQM teams. This activity may be co-ordinated at the steering committee level if the systems are to be used company-wide. This decision should be made at the planning stage.

6 *Develop TQM tools.* Education and training sessions will provide everyone in the organisation with the knowledge of how to use a series of tools to help them improve work processes. These tools include:

- Analysing work process flows
- Sub-process modelling
- Establishing customer, supplier and process requirements
- Attribute measurement
- Statistical process control

All these tools must be supported by documentation, measurement charts, requirement forms and calculating devices. It is the responsibility of TQM teams to select, design or otherwise make these supporting items readily available.

7 *Establish review procedures.* The Plan will have developed criteria and

benchmarks to measure the success of the TQM process. The TQM teams will be responsible to the steering committee for ensuring that regular reviews are carried out to measure progress against the criteria. These reviews will generally concentrate on measuring the implementation of systems and the use of tools in their area of responsibility. They may also include the conduct of attitude surveys and the use of other questionnaires.

A team may work with external consultants in carrying out these reviews or conduct their own reviews independently. However, early study of the Plan is important to establish the nature, procedures and frequency of reviews so that conducting them becomes an easy and natural part of the process. Senior management involvement in the review process is discussed in Chapter 31.

All the TQM actions described are to some extent regular and on-going. The systems and procedures developed by the various teams are in themselves work processes and can be continuously improved. Therefore the review process should examine the actions and outputs of the teams to see if they are fully effective and can be improved.

Improvement Actions

Management must provide leadership if the company objective of total continuous improvement is to be reached. Making rousing speeches declaring commitment or exhibiting 'walk-about management' are not leadership. In the words of the Roman Catholic catechism, they can be signs of 'inward grace' but are leadership only if inward grace actually exists. The obvious and oft-quoted examples are management actions which refuse to compromise on quality when the easy decision would be one that sacrifices quality to immediate revenue.

The best form of senior management action is to *insist* that their decisions on the implementation of TQM are carried out throughout the organisation and then actively to *help* their people to carry them out. The first opportunity to demonstrate leadership has to be planned and designed into the process. This is the real purpose of what may be termed the *improvement actions*. These actions associated with the improvement process can be summarised as follows:

1   Insist that all managers complete their education as scheduled.
2   Select three key company work processes for analysis and establish management teams to carry out the analysis.

3 Define work process improvement goals and review departmental organisation and objectives in the light of quality.

4 Transfer ownership of work processes to line management.

5 Insist that line management ensure that all employees complete their education as scheduled.

6 Insist that customer, supplier and process requirements are defined and published for *all* work processes.

7 Conduct departmental and process management reviews to ensure that opportunities for improvement are defined.

8 Conduct reviews of the TQM process to ensure that total ownership of the process can be transferred to line management.

These actions are designed to make certain that the new culture is fully absorbed into the 'woodwork' of the company – that continuous improvement is the normal way of conducting business. On the way to this objective, management will need to take many other actions to maintain the impetus (some of these are described in Chapter 31). Above all, quality must become the first objective. Do that and all the other objectives will have a much better chance of being achieved.

Following are some guidelines for each of the improvement actions summarised above:

1 *Insist that managers are educated.* In every company in which the authors have been involved, there have always been busy managers who had a good reason to miss their scheduled quality education. In some cases they have attended some sessions but tried to delegate other sessions to a subordinate. Many insisted that they were fully committed to quality and already understood the improvement process because of the books they had read. In our experience the progress of quality improvement is always slowest in the departments of managers who take this attitude. They give a clear message to their people as to where they place their priorities, and their people naturally follow their example.

These same managers would not dream of missing a meeting called by the managing director or their immediate boss. However important their other activities are to the organisation, senior management must insist that they attend the quality education scheduled for them. This is the first demonstration of commitment and constancy of purpose by the company's leaders. It must be made clear that no matter how highly the individual's contribution to the company is valued, he must abide by company decisions. Of course there are occasions when illness, accident or other external events can interfere with the educational plan, but these events should be catered for as much as possible in the scheduling.

2 *Select three key work processes.* Typically, organisations involved in quality improvement start by selecting their ten top problems. This is often
the result of a brainstorming session by a group of senior operational
managers. But quality problems are caused by the failure of work processes to meet the requirements (often because they are not defined) of
their customers. For every work process that is brought into a state of
control, hundreds of so-called problems disappear.

Even if management initially find it easier to use the language of
problems, they must then stop and determine which set of interconnected work processes the problems derive from. The next step is to select
three key work processes which in their opinion will have the most
impact on improvement. With a little thought it becomes obvious which
processes should be chosen. Typical choices are billing, sales order
processing or new product introduction from concept to launch.

This action cannot sensibly be started until a substantial number of the
management team have completed their TQM education. They will need
a comprehension of the concept of work processes and the communication of requirements before they can 'think processes' rather than
problems. In time all work processes must be analysed and brought into
a state of control so that their performance can be predicted and their
improvement planned. However, a whale has to be eaten in small bites
and Rome was not built in a day, etc, etc.

Once the key work processes have been selected, the management
team should appoint a senior member of management who will be given
the resources and authority to establish a team of managers to analyse
the flow of connecting and interconnecting processes involved. This will
establish a process-flow map showing how the network of processes
extends through company departments. Alternatively, external consultants (with work process knowledge) can be engaged to carry out this
first analysis.

The analysis usually throws up some interesting issues. Typically, it
will reveal that some processes in the network are duplicating the work
of others, some process outputs are being validated with parameters that
bear no relation to the output requirements of those processes, and
generally there is little communication between processes. The problems
of fortress management and the over-the-wall syndrome become very
apparent at this stage.

The objective of the team in analysing the process flows is to establish
clear task or sub-process boundaries (customer-process-supplier links)
and provide recommendations. The relationship between departmental
boundaries and process boundaries should also be mapped and documented. The team does not have the responsibility for implementing
improvement actions, so their work is completed with the submission of
their report to senior management.

3 *Define work process improvement goals.* The impact on senior management of the earliest of these analytical reports is usually enormous. To
date everything that they have learnt about quality has been concept or
theory; now they are faced with hard facts from their own organisation.
For example, readers of this book may well have accepted the concept
that management is vertical through departments while work processes
are horizontal and cross many departmental boundaries. However, the
authors would be amazed (though gratified) to hear that a reader had
immediately rushed out to re-organise his or her company on that basis.

The first realisation brought home to management by these reports is
that no one in the organisation has or accepts responsibility for the whole
process that they describe. In reality, so many are responsible that no
one individual *can* accept responsibility. In manufacturing processes an
overall responsibility is sometimes established, but it almost always
proves to be non-existent in the administrative processes.

The second realisation is that it is not in any one individual's interest to
accept responsibility for the whole process. The manner in which management objectives are set and individual managers are measured
actively *prevents* departmental managers from exercising any responsibility for processes not under their direct control or part of their defined
objectives.

The third realisation is that the process network, as presently operating, is not a chain of processes always meeting internal customer
requirements and therefore is highly unlikely to delight the external
customer. There are too many weak links.

These realisations provide the opportunity to define a series of
improvement goals. These are likely to include a review of the present
organisation and departmental goals. Before dramatically changing the
whole company organisation and the operational goals, however, it
might be wiser to select further processes for analysis so that a whole
picture emerges. The key improvement goals at this stage should relate
to the processes that have been analysed.

4 *Transfer ownership of work processes.* This particular improvement action
is the crux of the whole improvement process. In time this one decision
by senior management will lead to a whole new management style.
Managers will concentrate their efforts on systems rather than automatically blaming employees for everything that goes wrong. The natural
follow-through will do more to establish co-operation and harmony in
the workplace than any other personnel philosophy. Management will
also find that the payback is enormous, because they will at last release
the potential of their employees to contribute to improvement and
innovation.

The immediate decision required is to appoint managers to take responsibility for each of the processes that have been analysed. They will have responsibility for the improvement goals that have been established. Their responsibility will cross all related departments and functions as determined by the work process map. A new understanding of the complete business process will grow, and steadily more and more work process flows will receive this management attention. The series of individual links in the chain of processes will receive co-ordinated attention.

A member of the author's consultancy team once humorously entitled this approach 'chain gang management', but perhaps chain *team* management is not an inappropriate title for this management style. IBM have been pioneers in this approach, and their experience has been well documented in the writings of H. James Harrington referred to in the bibliography of this book.

5 *Insist that all employees are educated.* Some middle and supervisory managers will find reasons why this is not the appropriate time to train all the employees on their location. They will hold to this view even when they know that senior management has provided the recources for their education and training. The reasons will vary from the pressure of the current workload to the stated opinion that the workers are not interested or that 'they wouldn't understand the issues.'

Once again, senior management must insist that company policy must be adhered to without exception. The TQM organisation must be mindful of this situation in their education planning.

6 *Insist that requirements are defined.* This important improvement action has in reality started earlier, but can be completed when the education and training of everyone in the organisation has been completed. In the authors' experience all the members of a department or work group can enthusiastically discuss customer–supplier relationships and work process models in a classroom, yet do nothing differently in their workplace. Generally this is the fault of their manager or supervisor. He may have been equally enthusiastic when in the classroom, but claim that 'work pressures' or (in his view) higher priorities have prevented implementation of the concepts.

Even the smallest sub-process is a link in the chain. When everyone in the work group has been involved in defining and agreeing customer, supplier and process requirements, attitudes will change. All the requirements must be defined and published. This provides a basis for measurement and improvement. There can then be no misunderstanding – a requirement has been met or it has not been met.

Senior and/or process management must take the trouble to visit 'gemba' – the workplace – and satisfy themselves that this improvement action is being implemented. If it is not they must *insist* that it is commenced forthwith.

The reader will have noted that this is the third time we have used the word 'insist' in describing these improvement actions. The most difficult part of the whole process of change is to break traditional habits and the inertia of prevailing attitudes. Overcoming this inertia requires leadership which indeed *insists* that actions decided upon are actually carried out. Throughout this book the terms 'co-operative', 'participatory' and 'total quality management' have appeared. These terms are not similes for soft management. The authors' tendency is to believe that final decisions should always be made by an odd number, and that three decision makers is usually too many! In other words, teamwork should unearth all the options but one individual has to make the decision and stick by it. The whole exercise is pointless if management do not then insist that the decision is implemented. Consensus management is often settling for the lowest common denominator.

7 *Conduct departmental and process management reviews.* Management need to ensure that there is a continual review of progress in each department's contribution to improvement. A key factor is to examine the success of the matrix approach to processes and in that light consider the overall organisation of the company.

The company is now entering the sixth stage of quality improvement (see Chapter 5) – continuous improvement. Operational management at every level and in every function should be considering opportunities for improvement as part of their normal activities. These opportunities should be defined and from now on become part of the objective-setting and incentive system for management.

8 *Transfer total ownership of the TQM process to line management.* This is a difficult stage to assess. The overall objective of the TQM process is to make that process redundant. This will happen when total continuous improvement has become the natural management style and the new culture has been firmly established throughout the organisation. This may be many years away, so may not be a major concern at the outset, but its consideration does help to clarify the objective.

Despite everything you may have read, or is implied by the methodology of some quality gurus, it is worth noting that the leading Japanese companies do not have a quality management structure as it has been described here. They no longer need to manage the change! Quality has become equal to cost and schedule and is the natural priority for the whole organisation in its drive for continuous improvement and innovation.

However, it is time to return to the reality of the present western position and examine the issues of communication; the need to improve it at every level is the subject of the next chapter.

28   What's in it for me?

Communication is an essential element of TQM. Several chapters in this book have referred to the company environmental problems caused by bad or non-existent communication. In Chapter 24, an illustration (Figure 25) diagrammed the four-way communication culture required if an organisation is to make real progress in quality improvement.

An informal communication network already exists in any organisation. It works with incredible speed through a series of hubs such as the coffee machine, the canteen, the toilets and the switchboard. Information flows downward and sideways but very rarely upward – indeed senior management are often totally unaware of this network's existence. It feeds on people's need to know what is really happening in the organisation, and perhaps more important, what is about to happen. In one sense it is a highly effective communication system, but it suffers from the defect that the original message is often wrong or transmitted completely out of context. Thus the network can degenerate into a rumour factory which nevertheless has a very real effect on perceptions and attitudes.

The informal communication network can therefore be a threat to creating a shared culture of co-operation and participation. It cannot be eliminated, but it will be much less dangerous if there are alternative and effective formal channels of communication. These channels must be truly four-way and must create trust by answering the desire for truthful information. Perhaps the most important prerequisite for a truly four-way system is managers learning to listen. Unfortunately, the most common formal communication systems are not only predominantly downward-only but they tend to re-inforce fear. They are often used just for control purposes relating to objectives or operational failings. Fear and barriers to real communication inhibit change – 'keep your head down' becomes the motto in the company.

The first opportunity in the TQM process to establish improved formal communication comes when it is time to communicate the need for change throughout the organisation. When executives decide to change the strategy and management style of their organisation they immediately launch an awareness campaign to convince the employees of the need to change. The timing for initiating awareness was discussed in the last chapter, but there are other issues which need to be understood. Fundamentlly, these are *how* and *what* to communicate in order to encourage and facilitate change. But before dealing with the nuts and bolts of how and what to communicate, the TQM team need a good comprehension of the concepts of communication in the workplace.

Working with people is all about communication. Management has the role of breaking down the barriers to effective communication. Individual managers must:

- Initiate awareness of TQM and the need for improvement.
- Communicate about requirements within the work group and on behalf of the group with other departments or levels of management.
- Promote ideas.
- Help people get involved in the improvement process.

Figure 32 represents the key issues affecting all communication in the workplace.

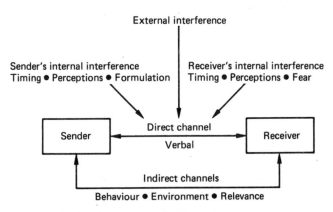

Figure 32   *Remove the barriers to communication.*

The key points made in the diagram are these:

- All communication is a two-way process.
- The most common direct channel of intended communication is verbal – words either spoken or written. They must be chosen carefully.

- Both the sender and receiver of messages create barriers or interferences that can obscure the intent of the message. These relate to their personal perceptions of the other party, their environment and the timing of the message. The sender must consider the likely effects of these things when formulating the message. Past company environment and objectives set earlier may also create fear in the mind of the receiver.

- External interferences must not be ignored when planning messages: A noisy environment for a meeting. Interruptions during a meeting. Inefficient mailing processes. A little thought can usually remove these barriers.

- Even when a message is sent directly, there are substantial barriers to reception and response. These can be seen as indirect communication. However strong the direct message, it will not enthuse if it is spoken with a hangdog expression and out of the side of the mouth. Equally, a memo about quality which contains misspellings and is badly copied will not have the desired impact. Most importantly, messages about quality from managers who do not practice what they preach will face insurmountable barriers.

- To maintain two-way communication the sender must also be a receiver. Ensure that the message was understood by asking questions, and above all, *listen* to the response.

The manager is the keeper of the communication trumpet. If he learns to play it well and make the right sounds, the fortress walls that stop communication will come tumbling down.

Communication and Motivation

When management start to communicate the need for change and the principles of TQM, they tend to speak in their own language and from their own perceptions. In fact a different language is used, and some different perceptions are held, depending on the individual's role in the organisation. The ability to receive any message will depend on the degree to which the mode of communication takes into account these differences in language and perception. This is all the more the case when people are being invited to change rather than just being given information.

Comprehension of the language issue starts with understanding the educational level of the recipient. Formal and social educational levels will affect the ability to comprehend concepts as well as actually understand the words used. This is not a patronising statement; it is a real fact of life which must be taken into account. Thankfully the concepts of TQM are commonsense and fundamentally simple – all they need is to be expressed simply. In many ways the principles are close to the aspirations of the average worker. However, there is a further language trap in business communications. In expressing need to change, the executive is likely to use the language of money. A good example is to mention the cost of non-conformance in the terms of percentage of revenue or operating costs. This comes naturally to executives as it was the language in which they were originally convinced. Workers tend to use the language of things or hours in their business life, such as the number of units or amount of time needed for an operation. Revenue does not mean a lot to people working on the shop floor. This is a normal barrier to communication in industry. Usually it is middle management who have to be 'bi-lingual' in communicating busines issues.

Even more important than language in business communication is the issue of what motivates people and their perceptions of the company and its management. There is a substantial body of literature on motivation, though interestingly enough most of it concentrates on the motivation of workers. The most influential (or certainly the most quoted) studies are the works of Herzberg on what gives people job satisfaction, McGregor's 'Theory X' and 'Theory Y' and the experiments of Elton Mayo in human relations in the factory as far back as 1933. This is not the place to discuss all the issues these authors have raised. However, a simple summation is that people (not just workers) are not motivated 'by bread alone', a view which was also held by some much earlier philosophers. In other words, though people are motivated by money and reward a more lasting motivation comes from a sense of achievement, from recognition that they count and from the satisfaction of the job itself. This view comes close to Deming's admonition to 'find joy in work'.

People's perceptions at every level of a company will affect their ability even to listen to motivational stimuli. Perceptions will be based on the history of the company or even the industry of which it forms a part. Previous management behaviour and the individual's role in the company will affect these perceptions and therefore affect reactions to communication. Redundancies, mergers, acquisitions and the history of industrial relations will all affect perceptions. At the apex of the organisational pyramid (the executives' level), where communication of the need to change originates, there is a tendency to view the organisation as monolithic or at least homogeneous in its culture and likely reactions. In fact the structure of most organisations is complex, and there can be substantial cultural differences and perceptions from location to location. A communications plan must take all these differences into account.

The evolution of industrial and commercial organisations has exaggerated the differences between people by dividing them into separate groups defined by role models which influence their behaviour. These roles, broadly speaking, fall into the following categories:

- Executives and senior operational management
- Middle management
- Professionals or knowledge workers
- First-level supervisors
- Workers (and their own subdivision, Staff)

Though these categories or roles can be divisive, to the extent that they have established behaviour patterns and perceptions which need to be surmounted, they are also all composed of *people*. The great opportunity for TQM lies in the fact that people all have similar motivations, though they may express them differently.

Attitudes are formed as the result of common and continuing experiences. The current attitudes in a typical large organisation will range from commitment (usually based on comprehension or knowledge) through both scepticism and cynicism down to apathy. Scepticism will be encountered in the middle management ranks and particularly amongst the knowledge workers. The latter often view themselves as a race apart from those whose jobs involve them in 'company politics' or managerial concerns. Cynicism is very apparent at supervisory level and among workers in particular roles. A good example of roles establishing cynicism is to be found in customer service engineers. They have been living directly with the daily hassle caused by faulty products. They have completed thousands of fault logs demanded by management, but nothing has changed. The rest of the organisation is generally apathetic. They just want to go through the day until they can escape the necessary evil of work and do something interesting to them. These attitudes are a terrible indictment of managerial practice over the years.

Attitudes can be changed by knowledge and new experiences and a reason to believe. Education and everyday communication will steadily develop knowledge. Behaviour and actions must support this knowledge to provide the new experiences. The change will take time (after all it took time to create the present environment), so a communication plan must be ongoing. The communicators must be aware of the barriers to communication but concentrate positively on the commonality of two main motivations shared by all.

The key motivator shared by everyone in the organisation is *pride*. Most people start by wanting to do a good job. They want to be proud of their personal contribution and to feel that others recognise that contribution, however small it may appear. Perhaps surprisingly, they also want to be proud of the company they work for; they want their family and friends to know that they work for a good company. To them the term 'good company' encompasses the product or service produced, the success of the company, the excellent management possessed by the company and the way the company recognises and treats its employees. There are outstanding companies in which all the employees share this pride. The author well remembers, when he was in the computer industry, the pride in their company exhibited by IBM employees at every level in the organisation. On the negative side, the very worst thing that one can ever do is to destroy an individual's pride. This is the first lesson for interrogators in a police state. Yet by default rather than intentionally, companies do damage the pride of individuals.

The second motivation shared by all is that people would like to ENJOY their work. This is as true of the worker on the shop floor as it is of the highest executive. Too often work is surrounded by hassle and stress which prevents joy in work. The TQM process must concentrate on removing the unnecessary hassle. Evidence of the truth of this assertion is all around us. Consider the host of retail and service organisations used by all of us in our everyday lives. Correlate the efficiency of service with the warmth of reception and the level of smiling amongst the staff of the organisations. Compare this with the service provided by the organisation that exhibits dourness and brittle tenseness. The same comparisons can be made between departments in individual companies. The authors believe that the measure of enjoyment people are getting from carrying out their tasks is an infallible guide to the measure of delight they give to their customers. These measures are also a good guide to the level of effective communication in the workplace.

Other motivations are present, such as the aspirations of the individual and the rewards that can be earned, but they tend to be pre-eminent for short periods only. Pride and enjoyment are lasting and continuous motivators. There are also negative motivators such as fear of the future, indeed fear for one's survival, and they will also need to be addressed.

The Communications and Awareness Plan

All these factors mean that awareness and good communication require careful and thoughtful planning. The plan should be based on knowledge, be on-going and exhibit a continuing integrity. Above all, avoid the temptation to 'beef-up' communication with short-lived hype. Clever promotional techniques in this area walk a thin line between drawing attention to the message and becoming the message itself. The latter approach is doomed to failure and will receive the reaction, 'Here we go again.'

The efforts made from the outset in the assessment and planning stages of the TQM process are ideal preparation for the planning and implementation of improved communications. The assessment phase will have provided some insights about perceptions and attitudes at varying levels of the organisation, while the planning stage provided the knowledge that has to be communicated.

The communications and awareness plan must be developed to fit the culture of the overall organisation and reflect the differences that may exist in different locations or functions of the company. This means that awareness programmes should not commence until the senior locational management have been educated. Knowledge will need to be supported by explanation to ensure that comprehension gradually overcomes prevailing attitudes. The amount of knowledge released at each stage must be related to the progress of the TQM and improvement actions and the cascading-down of education and training. There is always a danger that a catalogue of concepts or systems and tools will mean very little to people and may just confuse them. The major facts and ideas to be communicated can be summarised as follows:

- Quality improvement is now a major priority of the company. (This should be supported by the quality policy.)
- There are good competitive reasons for this change of emphasis.
- *Everyone* will be involved in quality improvement, and the first to be educated in it will be the managers and supervisors. (Support that management must first get its act together.)
- An important element of this plan will be an understanding of the company mission and the principles and values which will foster company-wide co-operation. (Support this by publishing the agreed mission principles and values.)
- The concept of the internal customer and the importance of communicating requirements will be explained and put into practice throughout the company.
- When management and first-line supervisors have completed their education, everyone else will be educated to play a part in the improvement process. (Support this by discussing employee education and announcing the suggestion system explained in Chapter 30.)
- Everyone will be allowed to express their point of view. (Continuously reinforce the concepts, principles and values. Support them by examples and success stories, and by encouraging everyone to express their ideas.)

- Customer orientation is to become a reality, not just a slogan, and the company will learn to delight the customer with continuing improvements and innovations.

Communication involves choosing from a myriad of techniques and opportunities. The choices will depend on the structure and nature of the organisation involved. In considering the techniques available there are some guidelines which should be helpful.

- Pronouncements must be supported by discernible action. Actions speak louder than words.
- Motivational programmes alone do not have lasting effect. For example, posters can support attitudinal change but they will not in themselves create the change.
- Communication is a continuous exercise and should steadily become a normal part of the business environment and not just a TQM activity.
- One-to-one communication can be the most effective as long as *listening* is a key component.
- In the perception of the average worker, senior management starts with his immediate supervisor's boss. He feels little empathy for the company's chief executive if he works for a large company.
- Recognise people or groups for their contributions. Always recognise them by name, not just location or department.

The warnings we gave earlier about hype or razmatazz do not preclude the use of imagination or humour. In fact cartoons and humour generally are very powerful conveyors of ideas and concepts. It must not be forgotten that one of the objectives of achieving open and frank communication is that people should enjoy their work. The process of change should bring a degree of fun into the working environment. Some common approaches used to communicate awareness are as follows:

- Hold company and department meetings.
- Send letters to all employees, perhaps included with payroll letters.
- Publish articles in company periodicals or develop a new periodical specifically dedicated to improvement.
- Show videos and films.
- Display the quality policy, mission statement and the principles and values on notice boards and at other visible points throughout the organisation's facilities.
- Place articles in the local press and industry or trade magazines.

- Publicise the improvement process in all company brochures and external statements.
- Involve people in the design of posters and cartoons and the provision of photographs.
- Include TQM on the agenda of every management or company meeting.
- Ask people for their experiences, opinions and ideas.
- Support all TQM measures and improvement actions with well-presented explanations before implementation and publicise success after implementation.
- Depending on the environment, use any of a vast number of promotional artefacts as reminders that this is an ongoing process.

Communication needs planning, but it also needs feedback. Be sure that the message sent was the message received. Measure changes in perception and attitude. The communication process itself can be continuously improved. The other arm of communication, namely education and training, will be discussed in the next chapter.

29   Back to school

Education and training are an essential element of the TQM process. In Chapter 26 the broad objectives of the education plan and some of the timing issues were addressed. This chapter will mainly concentrate on the content of the syllabus. The education plan is a major demonstration of a company's commitment to taking quality improvement seriously. It is unlikely that the employees have previously seen this level of investment in their development. This investment is heavy, both in financial terms and in employee time, and it is therefore important that careful thought be given to organisation and content.

There is a distinct difference between education and training. Parents, for example, would probably exhibit little concern in today's world to learn that their children will receive sex education as part of the school curriculum. There would be a different reaction if the school announced that they would also receive sex training! Education in quality improvement is about understanding the concepts and principles. Training is about learning practical skills. In one sense education is about *why* we do something and training is about what to do and how to do it. Education should create the environment in which employees are motivated to implement improvement in practice.

Education and training was classified in Chapter 27 as a TQM action, but it must support the improvement actions as well. The type and content of courses used in the TQM process divides them into those helping people to manage the change and those helping people to manage quality improvement. Figure 33 illustrates this point. A nucleus of people in the company have been selected as facilitators for education and training in the TQM process or the management of change. They will learn about the concepts that lie behind managing quality and the planning of the TQM process. At this stage they are learning about managing the TQM process rather than managing quality. Every employee, including the nucleus, will be included in the education and training for managing quality.

There is a wide variety of education and training courses available

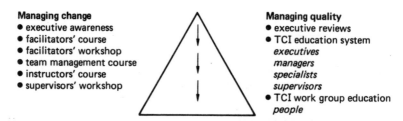

Managing change
- executive awareness
- facilitators' course
- facilitators' workshop
- team management course
- instructors' course
- supervisors' workshop

Managing quality
- executive reviews
- TCI education system
  executives
  managers
  specialists
  supervisors
- TCI work group education
  people

Figure 33   *Educating and training for TQM – typical courses.*

internationally which deal with all aspects of quality improvement. They vary in organisation and content, and unfortunately they also vary in quality. Some concentrate on specific techniques such as statistical process control (SPC) and design of experiments. Several reputable consultancies and educational establishments concentrate on the broader educational elements of the whole TQM process. Philip Crosby Associates (now part of the Proudfoot organisation) have established Quality Colleges throughout the world to teach the concepts of the founder, Philip Crosby. The Deming and Juran Institutes have approved other consultant organisations to teach the respective philosophies of these gurus.

Presumably to maintain the integrity of the gurus' original ideas, these courses hardly vary from country to country, though printed materials are translated and videos dubbed into diffent languages. This aproach has both advantages and disadvantages. The advantages, particularly the uniformity of standard and content, are obvious to a big international corporation. The disadvantage is that such 'packaged' courses take little account of the cultural difference between countries and between companies. This can throw up barriers to communication.

The dilemma for the company planning its educational approach is that at this relatively early stage in the development of TQM there are very few consultants or educators available with the necessary knowledge and experience. Almost certainly they will not exist in the company's own education and training department. These in-house people may be capable and dedicated, but they are part of the current culture and have little experience of the desired culture. They will not get sufficient knowledge to change people's minds by just reading the gurus' books. These are the main reasons why companies tend to select packaged education from the guru of their choice. It does have the merit of being available, though it can be very expensive.

Over the years the authors have attended many courses on quality improvement, including those of the main gurus. As a result we have developed strong views of what is required, both in content and method of approach. From our own experience we have developed the following principles which guide our approach to quality education and training:

- Education and training should be tailored to the organisation's culture and *its own plan* for the implementation of TQM.
- Education particularly requires tailoring. This is not to suggest that the company has to re-invent the wheel; education materials may be based on a generic model but amended or added to in key areas to assist communication. For example, the policies, mission, values and principles developed at the planning stage should form an integral part of the educational course content.
- Education and consultancy are inextricably linked. Many managers return from quality improvement courses and then have difficulty implementing the theories discussed in the classroom. They need help. This is particularly important at the outset of TQM implementation.
- Only a certain amount of knowledge can be assimilated, or practical skills developed, in one course. A series of relatively short sessions held at regular intervals and including assignments to be carried out in the workplace are infinitely preferable to a single solid week of coursework. This is particularly true of the education and training for managing quality.
- Education and training are on-going. As the process of TQM develops, many further techniques, skills or people-development needs and opportunities will appear. Education and training itself becomes an improvement action rather than a TQM action.

The content of available courses differs widely. This is not necessarily a criticism, as different approaches will suit different organisations depending on their present stage of awareness and culture. However, this variety does emphasise the importance of the assessment and planning stages in preparing for TQM. The TQM co-ordinator or the management team should evaluate the educational offerings of consultants or others. Again, do not delegate this activity to the training department. Key areas of the evaluation are assessing how well the content fits the organisation and how suitable it is for tailoring.

The consultants or educationalists are teaching students to be customer-conscious and to always meet the customer's requirements or needs. Insist that they practice what they preach and are prepared to develop or amend their materials to meet your company's requirements.

The content and organisation of the educational approaches described below are designed to support the TQM approach described in this book. The ideas are not set in concrete; they are being continuously improved and are designed to be tailored or customised to delight the customer.

Managing Change

Figure 33 listed courses designed to support the two educational streams. Executive awareness has been described in Chapter 26. The facilitators' course and workshop are designed to provide the knowledge necessary to develop the company's Quality Business Plan. All the elements of the Plan discussed earlier are included. At the end of the five-day course the facilitators, either individually or in groups, are set assignments to prepare components of the plan. These tasks are not an exam, so consultant assistance should be provided to help with the assignments. The linked workshops are held some two to three weeks later to bring the components together into a co-ordinated Plan for final approval by the Quality Steering Committee.

The first TQM action following approval of the Plan is to establish TQM teams as defined in the organisational section. The team course is designed for members of these teams. The content should include the concepts of TQM and discussion of the elements of the Plan that they will be responsible for implementing. This course will be similar to the facilitators' course, but by definition it has to be a course developed in collaboration with the facilitators.

The primary coursework for the managing-quality stream should be given by in-house instructors, preferably selected from management. These are not necessarily full-time appointments. These instructors have to learn how to use the material and will need help in organising session and in general teaching methods. This is the purpose of the instructors' course: to ensure that they have a good knowledge of TQM principles and the company's plan for implementing them.

The education plan also should provide for a short workshop for supervisors to equip them to use the material for work-group education and training. Following the 'cascading' principle, this activity will not commence until management in the location have received their own education. This is an important principle, as management and first-line supervisors have a major role in helping people as they start their own direct involvement in the improvement process.

Managing Quality

A TQM education system is a principal agent of change in management behaviour, introducing both new attitudes and the practice of new skills. Management must wholly understand the concept of work processes and their responsibility to ensure that these processes are in a state of control. This requires that classroom work be closely allied with practical application in their own operations. This is unlikely to be achieved in off-site intensive single courses. A better approach is to schedule regular modules spaced approximately one week apart. Each module will develop a concept or teach a skill in learning and workshop sessions. This knowledge should then be applied through work assignments, reviewed and then added to in the next module. A possible content for these modules is described later in the chapter.

The TQM education system proposed here is designed to be modular and can be varied to suit company education plans. A 'cascading' schedule needs to be developed to include the following categories of students, in the order in which they are listed:

- *Executives*: They have to know how to develop the new environment and the common language that henceforth will be used in the company. It is also an indication to everyone of their commitment.
- *Managers*: They will represent the 'engine room' of the TQM process. Successful implementation lies on their shoulders.
- *Specialists*: The importance and special characteristics of this group have been stressed before. They need to be brought into the fold.
- *First Line Supervisors*: They have direct contact with the workers and the future will depend upon them. There are a wide variety of titles used to represent this group; one definition for supervisors is those individuals who are empowered to change the pattern or allocation of other peoples work.

A major danger in selecting different education systems for the last two categories is to artificially divide people between staff and hourly paid employees. The pride and effectiveness of highly skilled and responsible hourly paid employees is often damaged by educational programmes which appear to label them as lesser beings. What people do rather than how they are paid should be the guiding principle.

A working TQM education programme which is especially effective in administrative departments and service organisations is summarised below. The suggested content of the individual classroom sessions is sometimes supplemented by additional sessions which develop a specific technique further. This is another advantage of using a modular approach, with sessions built around these topics:

1 An introduction to the concepts of TQM, why the company perceives the need to change and student perceptions of their reasons to change.

2 Sharing the company mission, quality policy and the principles and values which the executives have stated as the future basis for the company.

3   Introduction to the concepts of work process flow, internal-customer requirements and interdependencies.

4   Further explanation and discussion of the issues surrounding the establishment of requirements.

5   The concept of measurement as an aid rather than an obstacle. An introduction to statistical concepts and the practical application of simple attribute measurement.

6   The principles of corrective action and the importance of identifying the root cause. Description and use of the company's corrective action system.

7   Developing the power of teamwork and simple problem-solving techniques. Many companies include courses on this subject in their normal education and training schedule. This session is therefore optional or can be integrated into quality improvement training.

8   Removing the barriers to communication and other elements of the manager's role in TQM.

9   Further study of statistical concepts. The reduction of variation and introduction of innovation. This session is often supplemented by further practical working sessions on statistical process control and charting.

10 A final review of the course, the company Business Plan and the systems available to help the students implement improvement. This session also provides an opportunity for a senior manager to discuss his commitment and answer student questions.

As the TQM education and training cascades down the organisation at each location, comprehension amongst managers and supervisors will become great enough to justify involving everyone else in the organisation. The awareness activities, meanwhile, will have been steadily preparing the environment for this moment. Advantages will be gained in the TQM education by conducting sessions with employees representing a variety of departments or functions. It is suggested that natural work groups should be the mix for the next phase. The suggested sessions have a heavy reliance on workshop activities and therefore need a different style of leadership.

This particular system has been divided into six sessions of approximately one and a half hours duration. Coming after the explanation above of the subjects for TQM education, the topics for work group education which follow are largely self-explanatory:

1   Introduction to TQM and principles and values

2   Work group processes

3   Meeting of requirements and group measurement

4   Problem solving and group teamwork

5   Corrective action and communication in the workplace

6   Company processes and the suggestion system

The intention of this chapter has been to provide a guide to the typical content of TQM education and training and to emphasise the importance of planning education to fit the organisation. The next chapter delves deeper into helping people get involved in the process.

30 *Good idea – but get on with your work!*

This book may appear to make scathing criticisms of management and their customary ways of dealing with other employees. The authors are indeed antagonistic to the *systems* that are typically used to communicate with employees, but we wholly recognise that the results are not the intention of managers. A very large number of managers, in our experience, are motivated to encourage teamwork, participation and good communication with employees. Unfortunately the corporate culture imposed on them, which they in turn pass on to others, negates these good intentions. The simplest of examples is that employees always (as managers see it) want to communicate at 'inconvenient' times when the managers can't listen because they are under pressure to meet a schedule or have to concentrate urgently on reducing costs.

If the environment can be changed and the hassles burdening management can be reduced, there is then time for communication. The real change comes about when managers realise that co-operation and communication will reduce aggravation all round and make their jobs more satisfying. The teamwork concept has to embrace the company, the management and the people; this is really the essence of TQM and essential to its establishment. The four key requirements of the TQM process are these:

- There must be a common understanding of quality and of the need to change.
- Management must develop operating principles and values which create the environment for continuous improvement.
- Management must create the organisation and provide the resources to support the improvement process.
- Everyone must contribute to the end product or service used by the customer.

In essence, the TQM process builds on a management commitment to change their own behaviour and their company's culture to establish a company-wide partnership of interest in total continuous improvement (Figure 34).

Figure 34   *Management must make it happen.*

Management must carefully plan the education and training needed to help establish the new environment. Step by step, everybody in the organisation must be educated and trained to use the systems and tools that will make the change happen. At each step, as managers and then the people start participating in making TQM happen, there must be an open communications channel for feedback to management about the progress being made. Remember that if the company is to move towards TCI, each individual has to make continuous improvement an essential element of all their activities. Feedback may indicate a need for improvement in the next stage of education, for example, or in the actions taken to make it happen. The role of managers and people in this partnership is the subject of this chapter.

Specific actions by management in partnership with people are needed to ensure that the environment truly changes. These actions can be categorised as follows:

- Leadership
- Communication
- Participation in establishing requirements, measurement and goal setting

- Providing systems for corrective action and improvement suggestions
- Recognition

Leadership and Communication

These two categories of management actions were discussed in some detail in Chapter 28, but it is worthwhile highlighting these two areas in the context of this chapter.

The aspect of managerial behaviour that will contribute most to breaking down barriers is the ability to listen. Many managers are not good listeners; they tend to believe that it portrays weakness. In their view they demonstrate leadership by knowing what needs to be done and issuing directives. However, TQM principles recognise that everyone wants to do a good job and that the person doing the job usually knows most about the job. If this is true, these people must have an opportunity to express their opinions. Management must use meetings and visits to the workplace as opportunities to ask questions and really listen to the replies.

The integrity of the quality improvement process really comes down to the integrity of the managers. If they compromise on quality in any of their own actions they will compromise and possibly destroy the whole process. Rather than one great initiative, the integrity of the manager is demonstrated by a thousand little actions such as:

- Practising good personal housekeeping
- Starting and finishing meetings on time
- Agreeing requirements with their own process customers and meeting those requirements
- Using measurement in their own processes
- Establishing quality goals for their own activities

A major temptation which management must resist is that of 'tampering with the process'. Tampering can be major or minor interferences with people working in processes. These managers believe that they are anticipating problems; statistical demonstration shows that in reality they are more usually sending a stable process wildly out of control and creating frustration for all around them.

Establishing Requirements

The need for senior management to insist that requirements are established for every work process was emphasised in Chapter 27. Operational management should work with their people to ensure that the process customer's requirements are fully understood, agreed and then made known to all those involved in the process. Once this has been done, requirements can be established for suppliers and for the process. It is a TQM requirement that this approach be applied to every work process within a manager's domain. This exercise in itself will encourage teamwork, a better understanding of what needs to be done and effective communication between work groups.

Measurement

A major criterion for evaluating the company-wide success of the improvement process is the degree to which measurement of work processes has been implemented. Education will develop the concept of measurement as a helpful tool and provide the competence to use it. Managers must ensure that measurement is being effectively implemented in all the work processes. The management actions required to fulfil this responsibility are as follows:

- Ensure that relevant charts and systems are available.
- Ensure that people working in a process fully understand the value of measurement and how to accomplish it.
- Help people working in a process select the most relevant elements in the process for measurement.
- Ensure that charts are displayed and that the measurement data collected is communicated and then used to encourage improvement.
- Ensure that the subject of measurement is processes, not people.
- Demonstrate their commitment to improvement by measuring their own work processes.

Goal Setting

The establishment of measurement should lead rapidly to the development of individual or group improvement goals. Management must ensure that employees are aware of the objectives of goal-setting and help them set and attain their own improvement goals. Everyone involved in the process should participate in formulating the goals so that they can feel a strong personal interest in the success of the drive to meet them. These are the key requirements for setting attainable goals that no one will regard as having been unfairly imposed on them:

- Goals must be measurable.
- Goal achievement periods should be relevant to the process.
- Goals should be achievable and not over-ambitious.
- Goals should be clearly displayed.
- Goal-setting must be participated in by everyone concerned.
- Goal achievement must be recognised.

Corrective Action

Individuals and/or departments will call for corrective action from the start of the awareness programme. People will have known about problems in their workplace before the advent of TQM and will see this as a chance to start corrective action and an early opportunity to test the company's commitment to improvement. This movement will accelerate as more employees become involved in the educational process.

TQM management must therefore ensure that a corrective action system is developed for the company. Operational management must help everyone to use the system properly and ensure that it is available to all. They also need to explain priorities and ensure that those involved are aware of progress. It should be noted that a documented system is primarily a device to handle those problems that cannot be solved immediately by first-line supervisors.

Conceptually, corrective action is a four-stage process:

1 Definition of the problem
2 Immediate, but short-term, fix of the problem
3 Identification of and corrective action on the root cause of the problem
4 Measured feedback of the process to ensure that the problem has been solved forever

Figure 35 illustrates that this is a closed-loop process. The measured feedback is related to the definition to ensure that the original problem has actually been solved.

A typical company corrective action system is illustrated in flow chart form in Figure 36. The company system should be integrated into the training material to ensure that all know how to use the system effectively. Managers and supervisors should encourage use of the system and help people complete forms or use other means devised to activate it.

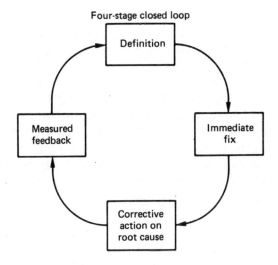

Figure 35 *Closed loop corrective action.*

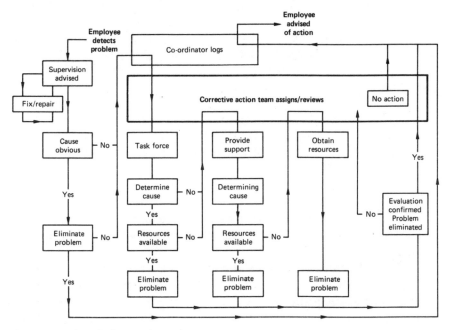

Figure 36 *A typical corrective action system.*

Suggestion Systems

Western industrialists have been staggered by the success of suggestion systems in Japanese industry. Yet again the approach was learnt from the Americans, steadily improved, and perhaps most important of all, driven by a committed management. The Training Within Industries (TWI) movement introduced in 1949 by the US occupation forces (before the advent of Deming and Juran) started the modern Japanese suggestion system. They were slow to get off the ground, though, until management began encouraging small work groups to both provide and actually implement suggestions. This small-group approach was really the precursor of the quality circle, which first appeared in 1962. Quality circles were really the result of a *Kaizen* approach by management. Now the suggestion system is an integral part of Japanese management. Indeed, the number of suggestions from a work group is a key criterion in measuring management performance.

The level of suggestions in Japanese industry *and* in Japanese companies in the West is vastly greater than in Western-managed businesses. The Toyota Motor chairman Eiji Toyada said in an interview, 'One of the features of the Japanese workers is that they use their brains as well as their hands. Our workers provide *1.5 million* suggestions a year and *95 per cent* of them are put to practical use.' This is really releasing the potential of the workforce to a degree not common in the West.

In his book *The Key to Japan's Competitive Success*, Masaaki Imai quotes Kenjiro Yamada, managing director of the Japan Human Relations Association, as stating that the suggestion system should go through three stages:

> In the first stage, management should make every effort to help the workers provide suggestions, no matter how primitive, for the betterment of the worker's job and the workplace. This will help the workers look at the way they are doing their jobs.
>
> In the second stage, management should stress employee education so that employees can provide better suggestions. In order for the workers to provide better suggestions, they should be equipped to analyse problems and the environment. This requires education.
>
> Only in the third stage, after the workers are both interested and educated, should management be concerned with the economic impact of the suggestions.

Yamada considers that this means management must think of the suggestion system in terms of a five-to-ten year span. Experience with Japanese companies in the West, for example the Nissan plant in Sunderland, UK, would indicate that Western workers may be able to adapt to the system at a faster pace, but as Yamada points out, Western companies encounter difficulties because they usually try to skip stages one and two and move straight to the third stage.

Japanese companies use financial incentive award schemes to encourage the continued input of suggestions. Many use complicated grading systems to evaluate the level of reward. These grading systems can use qualitative appraisal of both the level of creativity, originality, adaptability, etc, and the type of suggestion, from making the job easier to saving time and cost. The resulting points may then be multiplied by factors relating to the individual suggestor's role in the company. For example, the points could be multiplied by a factor of 1.1 for a blue-collar worker and by a factor of 0.9 for a supervisor.

The Western company must develop suggestion systems to suit the nature of their business, the range of skills represented in their workforce and the participatory culture of their company. They would be wise to also remember Yamada's three stages. The bibliography in this book refers to sources for detailed descriptions of specific Japanese company systems to assist managements in developing their own systems.

Recognition

It is now an accepted management principle that individuals should be recognised for their contributions. Management and people share in this principle. Good managers all recognise contributions and show respect for individuals as a daily part of their behaviour. TQM principles encourage this frequent and informal recognition.

However, TQM practitioners differ on the need for formal company systems for recognition. The co-authors of this book differ to some degree on this issue. John Piggott believes that formal systems can be abused by management, are often seen as patronising to workers and do not really fit the UK culture. John Macdonald recognises these dangers but is mindful of a greater danger – that not all managers naturally exhibit the habit of recognition. He believes that the TQM process must be used to change management behaviour and that this is an important area for change. Each company or organisation must make its own choice.

The adherents of formal recognition systems argue that it is important that everyone be involved in the recognition process, both to heighten mutual awareness and respect and to emphasise that *all* employees contribute to delighting the customer. A formal company recognition system ensures that both management and workers are included as individuals in the programme.

A key feature of formal systems is that both nomination and selection for awards in the company recognition system are done by peers. The reason for this is that individuals tend to value peer recognition more highly. Management-nominated awards are often viewed with suspicion. Previous experience has led people to believe that management has a hidden agenda when making awards, or that the recipient is a 'teacher's pet'.

This chapter has highlighted the participatory role of management in creating teamwork and in breaking down the barriers to communication. The next chapter discusses how to maintain the impetus of the TQM process once the initial euphoria has worn off.

31   *Keeping on course*

Competitive pressure and a growing comprehension of the importance of quality have led a substantial number of companies in the USA and Europe to adopt quality initiatives with enthusiasm and commitment. Yet far too many of these organisations have experienced an unfortunate change of emphasis less than two years after they started. Quality has somehow become last year's priority. This chapter examines the need and the actions required to maintain commitment and enthusiasm over the long haul, despite what appear to be competing priorities.

There are three key elements involved in maintaining the impetus and ensuring that the quality improvement process keeps on the planned course:

- Maintaining senior management involvement
- Reviewing and auditing the TQM process
- Reviewing the Quality Business Plan

These elements are of equal importance. The process must be constantly attended to and stimulated. Quality improvement cannot be successful if it is treated as a programme – it is a continuous *process*.

Senior Management Involvement

Chief executives are responsible for the future of their business. They set the course for the organisation and it is their task to keep the organisation on course. From the outset it is clear that TQM is a *change* of course, so it should be equally clear that maintaining the impetus of change is the chief executive's responsibility. Senior colleagues will be involved and some actions may be delegated to middle management, but the responsibility stays at the top. Starting with enthusiasm, showing commitment and doing their best to talk quality at every opportunity, though important, is not good enough.

Executives must personally involve themselves in reviewing and auditing the improvement process at all levels of the company. External consultants can be very helpful at review stages, but it must be clear to the organisation that management reviews and audits are taking place. The best way to ensure that the process is reviewed is to establish the timing and content of reviews at the planning stage. Regular senior management reviews of progress against the company's Business Plan is a normal business process. In a similar manner, regular senior management reviews against the company's Quality Business Plan must be seen as the norm.

Reviewing and Auditing the TQM Process

The Quality Business Plan establishes the process by which TQM can be implemented throughout an organisation. The term 'process' has been used throughout this book. Sometimes it has been applied directly to TQM and at other times used to describe work. The authors hope that this use of the word has not been confusing to the reader, but it was not an accident. The implementation of TQM is in itself a work process. Reviewing and auditing this process is not unlike ensuring that other work processes are in a state of control and that their outputs can be predicted. Following initial assessment and analysis, the Plan defines the requirements of the process and establishes criteria for measuring the outputs.

The customer of the TQM process is the organisation as a whole. The objective of the process is to delight the customer, though the Plan recognises that this will take time. The Plan therefore establishes some interim goals to define the level of change to be achieved at certain stages of implementation. Figure 37 illustrates the concept. In the diagram a number of outputs from the process are defined. A quantitative goal should be established for each kind of output which will in effect represent the customer's (ie, the organisation's) requirements. The audit must measure the level of success in meeting these requirements. The goals for the behavioural outputs would have been established from the assessment-stage perception and attitude surveys. A review stage would require new surveys to measure the extent of change.

As the process continues over time, further outputs can be defined and new, improved goals established. Figure 37 notes some inputs to the process, and of course more of these can be added to define requirements to be met by suppliers. Where output requirements are not being met, the audit will be focused on the extent to which the input requirements have been

TQM process inputs	TQM process outputs	Customer requirements
• Mission, policy, and principles and values defined and communicated	• Work processes being analysed and defined, and ownership established	• Key processes complete; improvement goals defined
	• Measurement of processes being implemented	• One per department minimum
• All employees educated	• Corrective action being implemented	• Number of improvement goals met
• Systems for corrective action, measurement, suggestions and recognition developed and available to all	• Improvement suggestions	• Average per employee and work group
	• Management behaviour change	• Perception survey goal
	• Employee attitude change	• Employee survey goal

Figure 37 *The TQM process should be reviewed as a work process – some typical plan criteria.*

met. The purpose of the review is to ensure that corrective action can be taken if required and to establish new improvement goals. The authors favour review of the basic TQM system outputs and requirements rather than measurement of the reduction of waste or cost of quality. If measurements of TQM effectiveness show that the process requirements are being met, this success should soon lead to success in meeting the normal business financial goals.

We recommend that the first TQM review along the above lines should be scheduled for six months from the establishment of the locational TQM teams. Thereafter reviews should take place at quarterly intervals, or whatever period is normal for the business. These are all senior management reviews of the TQM systems rather than reviews of management and people. Achievement of goals is a subject for recognition and awareness. Success will breed success.

Quality Business Plan Reviews

The TQM process reviews are designed to help senior management keep the process on course and to provide a way of measuring progress towards transferring 'ownership' of the TQM process to line management. An early opportunity to start this process comes when it is time to reformulate the overall Company Plan. The original Quality Business Plan was developed on a project-planning basis to initiate quality improvement. The progress against the Quality Business Plan must be reviewed and an updated plan prepared. However, at this stage the Quality Plan will be integrated into the normal Company Business Plan. Quality is built into the way the business is run. A crucial element of this plan will be to establish new goals and criteria, find new themes for awareness and define new actions to be taken. This whole operation will give added emphasis to TQM and concentrate thought on it.

Areas for new themes and actions can be based on a heightened awareness of the customer. Though the first period of the implementation of TQM has highlighted the importance of the customer, both internal and external, most of the actions have been concerned with managing the change. The company should be steadily moving towards the concept of the customer-driven business. This will require actions and activities directed towards that specific aim. These actions should bring the external customer to the fore. Customer surveys and new approaches to maintaining customer contact, so that their changing needs are anticipated, is an area that will provoke thought and new plans.

A project element of the Business Plan which can be introduced at this stage, if it does not already exist, is to develop a defined system for the introduction of new products or services. To maintain management integrity in the TQM process, any new product or service introduced after the launch of TQM must demonstrate management commitment to the principles.

An earlier chapter described the traumas and compromises with quality all too often associated with a new-product launch. There are many stages in the launch of a new product from original concept to final delivery. Each of these stages involves an ever-widening number of functions, processes and people. Each provides opportunities for error but equally, if well planned, opportunities for improvement. Independent senior management review procedures defined for each stage, which are *empowered to prevent the new product moving on to the next stage* until the requirements are met, will have a salutary and positive effect on the future of TQM and the company. The review procedures will differ according to the nature of the company and its products and services. A typical set of review steps for a new manufactured product could be:

- Conceptual design review before release to engineering
- Engineering design review before release to production
- Production review before new product announcement

- Production review before first deliveries to customers

These reviews should include the engineering, production, marketing, finance and servicing implications. The review body must have managerial clout and the relevant technical experience.

Business Plan actions like these reviews, concerned with the future quality emphasis for the organisation, are positive factors in maintaining the impetus of change towards an environment of total continuous improvement.

32 We cannot do it alone!

Every business organisation is dependent on its external suppliers and customers. If a company is to achieve a sustained competitive advantage, both its customers and its suppliers must be involved in the company's TQM process. This is not an improbable objective, as both have much to gain from the company's improvement.

Delighting the final customer is the objective of the whole exercise. To achieve this lofty goal, a customer-driven company will take action to anticipate the customers' need and continually add that little extra to delight them. The nature of the actions or involvement with the customer will depend on the type of business. Service companies will differ from manufacturing companies; the type of service or product will also determine different types of involvement. A bank will approach its customers differently from a hotel chain. A manufacturing company serving a mass consumer market must plan its approach differently from a company manufacturing high-value capital goods. What should unite all these organisations is a determination to know and understand the needs of their customers.

For many companies the sales force should be a constant source of information on customers' perceptions of the company and their changing requirements. However, this will not be achieved by sending the sales force a memo urging them to ask the customer what he wants. Establishing real perceptions and requirements is a process of intelligent questioning and listening. The salesforce will need guidance, model questionnaires and probably training. In the long term this will be an infinitely better use of a salesman's time than chasing late deliveries or dispensing expense-account generosity in the name of 'establishing good customer relations'. Management has a part to play in encouraging and supporting the salesforce in genuine customer-relations activity and then listening carefully to the customer views they report. This requires close collaboration between marketing, sales and the research or product-development section of the company. A similar approach and communication chain should be established for the after-sales service operations.

Listening to customers seems particularly difficult for some companies. Customer complaints departments are often used to keep customers at a distance so as to not inconvenience executives. The staff are sent to customer-care courses to learn how to soothe irate customers, but little is actually changed to improve the real service. Executives address 'user conferences', extolling collaboration and open discussion, and then berate the marketing operation for allowing the conference to 'get out of hand' because some of the users openly raised their concerns over the current products. This attitude has to change; executives must ensure that the organisation actively seeks the customer's view.

Major service and retailing organisations need to understand and foster their customer 'interfaces', or points of contact. Marketing and other senior management must plan to establish continuing communication links with their interface workers. Bank cashiers, ticket clerks, hotel receptionists, enquiry desks and many similar occupations provide the organisation's primary interface with the customers. They could be a constant source of information if their views and experience were sought.

The kinds of organisations we are talking about often organise 'cheese and wine' customer receptions or open days. These are pleasant events which demonstrate the work and services of the company or branch. The authors have attended many such events, but can remember no occasion on which we were asked our views as customers on the service or product. Each such occasion was intended to enhance customer relations but each actually represented a lost opportunity.

In truth, the marketing operations of the majority of companies are now taking a greater interest in the views and needs of customers. Market research and consumer surveys are examples of the growing competition to satisfy customer needs. In considering their approach to customers, managers should try to reverse roles and consider their own position as a customer of their suppliers. Can their company help its suppliers correctly anticipate *its* needs? It is just possible that the suppliers have the same problems determining the needs of their customers.

Major corporations such as IBM, Ford and Marks & Spencer establish long-term relationships with their suppliers on the basis that they share common interests and goals. IBM refer to their suppliers as 'business associates'. These companies recognised years ago that pressuring suppliers on price with the weight of their buying power was counterproductive. Awarding purchase contracts on price alone inevitably meant compromising quality. A substantial proportion of the buyer's internal waste and defective production was actually being bought in from suppliers. These corporations also realised that a host of problems involving suppliers are caused by the ordering company.

A corollary to these realities is that partnerships of interest cannot be established with a horde of competitive suppliers for each product. How would the buying company react towards its own customers if orders were fragmented or switched arbitrarily to maintain price pressure? This approach ignores the cost of evaluating new suppliers and the time lost in changing from one supplier to another. Multi-supply also introduces greater variation into work processes and thus works against the objective of reducing variation. Companies committed to continuous improvement are demanding the same from their suppliers. The first step on that path is to move towards single sourcing and then help the chosen supplier to meet the buyer's objectives.

Supplier relations based on single sourcing demands careful selection of suppliers and then a co-operative approach to meeting common objectives. This entails open communication based on the concept that the supplier wants to do a good job – indeed, the supplier also wants to delight the customer.

Selection will obviously take into account financial and technical competence, but should be extended to consider the personality and culture of the supplying company:

- Will they be able to share similar principles and values?
- How do they value their workforce – what are their employee relations policies?
- What is their attitude to quality?
- Will they need help in implementing a TQM approach?
- Are they likely to make good long-term partners?

This approach will highlight areas in which the buyer can help the supplier. It is particularly important to help the supplier understand the processes in which the materials or parts are to be used. Once the supplying company fully understands its customer's needs, it can invest in better tooling or production methods. The supplier's own innovation and continuous improvement can assist the customer.

Collaboration between customer and supplier can be seen as an exercise in extending the TQM chain through the internal work processes of both companies. If this is so, everything stated in this book about TQM applies to both partners. According to Tom Peters, Ford recognised the importance of partnership with suppliers by taking full-page advertisements in the *Wall Street Journal* and *US Today* to praise their suppliers with superb quality records. Examples of this approach to suppliers are now appearing in Europe.

Quality involves us all – big organisations and small. It is now a global issue which is creating a new era in industry and commerce. Total continuous improvement is a management style which can help us all. Competitive global quality may be the measure of the task, but prosperity and joy in work can be the measure of our success.

In conclusion, the authors would be delighted to receive readers' comments on any of the issues raised in this book and to learn from their experience. They can be reached at:

Resource Evaluation Limited
Park Gate
21 Tothill Street
London SW1H 9LL
Tel: 071–222 1212

Acknowledgements

Many people around the world have helped with ideas, read and commented on the manuscript and assisted in other ways. Of course our wives, families and pets have contributed too, but we have dealt with them separately! Our formal thanks are due to our colleagues at Resource Evaluation Ltd, particularly Christopher Bielenberg, who had faith in our original concepts, and to the following, who contributed ideas and commented on the manuscript (but cannot be blamed for any shortcomings in the final result):

Robert Collins, Vice President for Quality, American National Can, Chicago; Harry Gibson, ever-present friend and a great eliminator of commas; Paul Hewlett of the Department of Trade and Industry; Bob Lawrie, Society of Motor Manufacturers and Traders; Scott Leek, quality consultant, Miami, Florida; Joe McNally, Vice President, Compaq Computer, Richmond, London; Clifford Norman of Associates in Process Improvement, Austin, Texas; Dr Faith Ralston, an early pioneering colleague at Honeywell and now owner of Ralston and Company, Minneapolis, Minnesota; David Steel of the Department of Trade and Industry; Sheila Stevenson of Oak Park, Illinois – a library of information; Jim Thompson, Manager of 3M Quality Institute, Minneapolis; Wendy de Walden, Walden Associates, London; and Linda Vincze of Winter Park, Florida.

A special 'thank you' goes out to Dr Jay Leek of Winter Park, Florida, who has meant quality from the first day that John Macdonald met him and is the *real* inspiration for an obsession with quality; Sarah Potts, who indexed our research (77 books and 2,800 articles) and word-processed the manuscript; Linda Rae Baldwin, who over a long campaign finally convinced John Macdonald that he could write (she has a lot to answer for!) and finally, Crystal Palace Football Club, who occasionally provided a much-needed diversion.

Further reading and references

Several hundred books have been published on the subject of quality. The following selection includes any books which have been referenced in the text and others that the authors have found helpful. The list has been organised alphabetically by author within broad interest areas.

Thought provokers

Blake, Robert R., and Mouton, Jane S., *The New Managerial Grid*, Gulf Publishing Company, 1978

Clutterbuck, David, and Crainer, Stuart, *The Decline and Rise of British Industry*, Mercury, 1988

Crosby, Philip B., *Quality is Free: The Art of Making Quality Certain*, McGraw-Hill, 1978

Crosby, Philip B., *Quality Without Tears: The Art of Hassle-free Management*, McGraw-Hill, 1984

Deming, W. Edwards, *Out of the Crisis: Quality, Productivity and Competitive Position*, Cambridge University Press, 1988

Drucker, Peter F., *The Practice of Management*, Heinemann Professional, 1989

Fritz, Robert, *The Path of Least Resistance; Learning to Become the Creative Force in Your Own Life*, Fawcett, 1989

Halberstam, David, *The Reckoning*, Bloomsbury, 1987

Juran, Joseph M., *Managerial Breakthroughs*, McGraw-Hill, 1965

Naisbitt, John, *Megatrends*, Futura, 1984

Peters, Thomas J., *Thriving on Chaos: Handbook for a Management Revolution*, Macmillan, 1988

Japanese experience

Imai, Masaaki, *Kaizen: The Key to Japan's Competitive Success*, Random House, 1986

Japan Human Relations Association, *The Idea book: Improvement Through TEI (Total Employee Involvement)*, Productivity Press, 1988

Japan Management Association, *The Canon Production System: Creative Involvement of the Total Workforce*, Productivity Press, 1987

Lu, David J., *Inside Corporate Japan: The Art of Fumble-free Management*, Productivity Press, 1987

Mizuno, Shigeru, *Company-wide Total Quality Control*, Quality Resources, 1987

Mizuno, Shigeru, *Managing for Quality: The Seven New Tools*, Productivity Press, 1988

Schonberger, Richard J., *Japanese Manufacturing Techniques: Nine Hidden Lessons in Simplicity*, Collier Macmillan, 1983

Implementation

Carlisle, John A., and Parker, Robert C., *Beyond Negotiation: Redeeming Customer-Supplier Relationships*, Wiley, 1989

Crosby, Philip B., *Running Things: The Art of Making Things Happen*, McGraw-Hill, 1986

Cullen, J., and Hollongum, J., *Implementing Total Quality*, Springer Verlag, 1988

Edosomwan, Johnson A., and Ballakur, Arvind, *Productivity and Quality Improvement in Electronic Assembly*, McGraw-Hill, 1989

Foster, Richard, *Innovation: The Attacker's Advantage*, Pan, 1987

Groocock, John M., *The Chain of Quality: Market Dominance Through Product Superiority*, Wiley, 1986

Hale, Roger L., *Quest for Quality: Strategies for the 1990s*, Rooster Books, 1989

Harrington, H. James, *The Improvement Process: How America's Leading Companies Improve Quality*, McGraw-Hill, 1986

Mann, Nancy R., *The Keys to Excellence*, Mercury, 1989

Moir, Peter W., *Profit by Quality: The Essentials of Industrial Survival*, Ellis Horwood, 1988

Oakland, John S., *Total Quality Management: International Conference Proceedings*, IFS Publications, 1989

Price, Frank, *Right First Time: Using Quality Control for Profit*, Wildwood House, 1986

Robson, Mike, The Journey to Excellence, MRA International, 1988

Robson, Mike, *Quality Circles: A Practical Guide*, Gower, 1988

Scherkenbach, William W., *The Deming Route to Quality*, Mercury, 1991

Schonberger, Richard J., *World Class Manufacturing*, Collier Macmillan, 1987

Stebbing, Lionel Edwin, *Quality Assurance: The Route to Efficiency and Competitiveness*, Ellis Horwood, 1989
Tse, K. K., *Marks & Spencer*, Pergamon Press, 1985
Walton, Mary, *The Deming Management Method*, Mercury, 1989
Zeller, H. J., *The Best on Quality*, C. Hanser, 1990

Professional and technical

Amsden, Robert T., Butler, Howard E., and Amsden, Davida M., *SPC Simplified*, Quality Resources, 1986
Feigenbaum, Armand V., *Total Quality Control*, McGraw-Hill, 1987
Hamilton, S., *A Communication Audit Handbook*, Pitman, 1987
Juran, Joseph J., and Gryna, Frank M., *Quality Planning and Analysis: From Product Development Through Usage*, McGraw-Hill, 1980
Juran, Joseph J., and Gryna, Frank M., *Quality Control Handbook*, McGraw-Hill, 1988
Juran, Joseph M., *On Planning for Quality*, Collier Macmillan, 1988
Taguchi, Genichi, *Introduction to Quality Engineering: Designing Quality into Products and Processes*, Quality Resources, 1986
Taguchi, Genichi, *System of Experimental Design: Engineering Methods to Optimize Quality and Minimize Cost*, Quality Resources, 1987
Wheeler, Donald J., and Chambers, David S., *Understanding Statistical Process Control*, Addison-Wesley, 1990

Index